D0035678

To Milly

Big Toot III the latest in a series of 'Big Toots' Walt and Milly Woodward used to cruise the waters of the Northwest and Alaska, is a 46 ft. wooden Ed Monk design the Woodwards sold in 1986. A noted journalist, Walt is the former owner and editor of the Bainbridge Review, was boating columnist for the Seattle Times for several years, and has contributed many columns to Nor'westing magazine.

Table of Contents

Preface

Because this is another one of those 'how-to' books, you are entitled to know why you should pay any attention to my alleged expertise. After all, before you read Arnold Palmer on golf, you first had to be satisfied that he had won umpteen national tournaments; before you embraced a Julia Child's recipe, you first were convinced that she had fluffed up untold numbers of successful Grand Marnier souffles.

Well, is this book just a Johnny-come-lately fake, or does it really have respectable antecedents? Fact is, this book was a half century in the making. It all began on a day in the fall of 1934 when, as a cub reporter for *The Empire*, the daily newspaper in Juneau, Alaska, I visited the high school classroom of a certain Mr. Riegel, the science teacher and, for my purposes, coach of the basketball team. We were well along in my interview on the prospects for the approaching season when the door of an adjoining classroom was opened. A tall, slim, red-headed female entered and said, "Excuse me, Mr. Riegel, may I use your pencil sharpener?" What happened thereafter is exposed in some detail in another book[*] I wrote. Suffice for here to say that in 1935, in Seattle, I married the gal and promised, in addition to the usual vows, that the

*BIG TOOT, the summation of 25 years of Woodward family cruising, is now out of print.

day would come when, in our own boat, I would take Milly on a sentimental cruise back to Juneau. That day was a long time coming. But it did arrive and, on July 7, 1982 (a tad tardy, I suppose, but only by some 47 years) I piloted our cruiser up to a float at Juneau, and Milly stepped ashore.

As the first chapter will make clear, this 'how-to' book is aimed at making it possible for an inexperienced skipper to cruise to Southeast Alaska without getting into too much trouble. Milly and I were well beyond three score and ten years of age when we made that 1982 round trip and, believe me, both of us were feeling our antiquity. We had to stay out of trouble. We did. Mostly. Then, just to prove it was no fluke, we made a second round trip cruise to Southeast Alaska in 1983.

After that, I felt I knew how to cruise to the Land of the Midnight Sun without rocking the boat too much. As a columnist for *Nor'westing*, the Pacific Northwest's magazine for pleasure boating, I mentioned my hunch to the magazine's publisher, Tom Kincaid. There is a book here, he agreed, but he warned that it must be written for the inexperienced boater; books on cruising to Alaska are a dime a dozen; my book, he said, would have to be the first definitive one that would help a novice make the trip. With that encouragement, I wrote the book. *Nor'westing* carried a considerable number of the chapters as monthly installments, and Tom and his good wife, Louise, associate publisher of the magazine, agreed to publish the book. Believe me, there is no debt like that of an author to a supportive publisher.

My list of debits neither starts nor stops with the Kincaids. In the first place, there had to be the inspiration, and that is why this book is dedicated to Milly, tenderly, with love and with deep appreciation of her courage, her patience, and her understanding. But if I have her high on the pedestal of my affection, she is up there with a red pencil; a hard-nosed English teacher, she has edited every word herein. My grateful, but ungrammatical, soul thanks her.

Then there are Althea and Walt Jolly, fellow members of the Poulsbo Yacht Club and owners of a cruiser named the *Hyas Siah,* which translates to 'far-away places'. The Jollys had made a Southeast Alaska round trip in 1980 and were anxious to go again in '82. Their invitation to run with them gave us the courage to try it. Literally, they led the way. They showed us how.

Part of our learning experience in '82 we also owe to Lucille and Frank Drury of Seattle. In their *Grumpy,* a determined 50-foot rebuilt Coast Guard patrol ship, they took us into the unbelievable wonders of many Chatham Strait inlets and around an exciting and well-named place called Cape Decision. We owe them much.

I also am indebted deeply to my good friend and fellow Bainbridge Islander, Eilert Eliasen, a genuine expert of Southeast Alaska navigation. He spent many hours carefully checking my words and suggested course lines.

Finally, and particularly if your co-skippers are well beyond 70 years of age, you must have a good crew. We were and are blessed with fine grandsons, with John and David in 1982, and with John and Jaime in 1983; Grandma and Grandpa thank them more than they ever will know. Lastly, but most certainly not least, there were, also as crew members in 1983, two 'in-laws', Marian and Bob Pratt, who share two other grandsons with us; we certainly are beholden to them, too.

So, you see, I really had very little to do with it. With all that wonderful help, how could I miss? At any event, here it is, a cautious 'how-to' book on getting to and from Southeast Alaska in a small craft. We did it. You can, too.

Good reading. And good cruising!

W.W.

Wing Point, Bainbridge Island

Preface to the Second Edition

The title has been changed a teensy-weensy bit, the official chart numbers in the appendix have been brought up to date, and some typographical goofs in the original printing have been corrected. That's all!

Other than those minor editing improvements, this still is exactly the same little book that has already helped many hundreds of skippers to get to and from Southeast Alaska without—if you'll excuse the expression—rocking the boat too much.

There is nothing more joyous for an author than to be told more copies of his book must be printed. Humbly, then, my deep thanks. But I will not leave it there. Tom Kincaid, my publisher, must share that gratitude with me, for he is the one who predicted that there would be a perpetual demand for a book that was written primarily for the inexperienced, perhaps timid, skipper yearning to pilot his own ship to the far away and fabulous waters of the midnight sun. Tom is quite a prophet.

He is more than that. An experienced mariner in both sail and power boats, he gave this book the acid test in 1988, propping it up on the bridge of his trawler *Nor'westing* as he wheeled his round-trip way between Puget Sound and Southeast Alaska. His conclusion: "Don't change a word!"

However, he really didn't begin to use the book in detail until he had cleared Port Hardy. He didn't have to; he has roamed the waters between the north end of Vancouver Island and Olympia, where this book begins its navigational advice. Ha! This greedy author, always hoping to boost the sale of his book, sees a little noticed point here. The first 76 pages of the book cover the courses from Olympia through Puget Sound and Deception Pass into the San Juan and Gulf Islands, across challenging Georgia Strait, to all the charming anchorages in Desolation Sound, and safely through treacherous Johnstone Strait to the north end of Vancouver Island. The first 76 pages are written in exactly the same detailed and cautious manner that is the rule for the balance of the book.

So...this 'Alaska' book could also be a useful aid to the skipper who has no present intention of cruising to Skagway. That's why the title has been changed just a bit.

There. That may sell another copy or two.

Welcome aboard!

w.w.

Blue Heron Pond, Bainbridge Island

To Alaska,
With Confidence

It is a cotton-pickin' shame that there are so many boaters who dream of cruising to Alaska via the Inside Passage, but who haven't the faintest idea of how to do it and, because of that lack of knowledge, delay or otherwise shy away from coming to grips with their dream, perhaps forever denying themselves a great adventure.

Up to now, little has been done about that sad situation. Most of us marine writers fail to recognize that there are many thousands of boaters who are not experienced and who, thus, remain timid when it comes to the dream of cruising to Alaska. Without meaning to do so, we ignore them; we write above them simply because we have forgotten, or don't like to remember, our own original timidity. A timid boater is not a coward. There is a big, big difference between being timid and being a coward. A coward lacks courage. A timid person only needs self-confidence.

I am firmly convinced that an inexperienced boater—a timid one, if you please—indeed can make the Southeast Alaska round trip safely with a minimal amount of discomfort. I am equally sure I can help. To do it, of course, I won't be writing for the experienced, weather-beaten skipper. I can't tell that fellow anything he doesn't already know, and I'm not about to bluff it to get his attention. He's welcome, of course, more than welcome, as a reader if he finds Woodward interesting, but he will discover that things have been reduced to the basics that he was taught, or learned, 'way back at the beginning of his boating career. This book's aim, then, is to supply self-confidence.

If I can hit that target, it will be a good thing, for the vision of cruising to Alaska is a dream worth having. Southeastern Alaska will give you lifetime memories of towering, jagged, snow-covered mountains rising from inland seas; leaping, splashing porpoises playing tag with your bow waves; rain, pelting so hard it sounds like a drummer beating on your cabin top; hot, bright, sunlit days; summer days that end, more than less, near midnight, and nights that become morning about four hours later; glaciers marching from the sea to far back into majestic mountains; icebergs that are as blue-white as any color photograph you've ever seen; huge, lumbering brown bears unafraid of you or anything else; great whales that breach and sound; Juneau's Red Dog Saloon, and Ketchikan's former bawdy houses lining Fish Creek with the naughty reminder that the creek was once the only place in the world where both fish and fisherman went upstream to spawn; beautiful, historic Sitka, glorying in its native and Russian past behind a score of charming, tree-covered islands; bustling Petersburg where herring can be jigged by the bucketful from almost any float; huge tourist ships; graceful kayaks, and more, much, much more ...

So let me give you the confidence to turn that dream into a reality you'll never forget. Why me? I have only a few credentials, but they may qualify me for the task.

In the first place, I have been cruising in a motley collection of powerboats for more than 30 years. In an outboard-propelled 21-foot cruiser (Ha! But that's what the salesman said it was even though, at night, you had to shove two recumbent bodies aside to go to the head), I packed one wife, three daughters and one large dog, and went from one end of Puget Sound to the other, and into the San Juan and Gulf Islands. In a gasoline-powered, single screw, 34-foot raised deck craft, the Woodwards explored Desolation Sound in Canada many times and, during one memorable summer, Milly and I braved a succession of huge locks in the Columbia and Snake Rivers, reaching to within 47 miles of the Idaho state line before we decided we had plowed through enough searing hot wheat fields. And, in *Big Toot III*, a 46-foot, twin screw diesel-powered ship, we twice—in 1982 and 1983—made Inside Passage round trips to Southeastern Alaska.

Secondly, in those three decades, I have managed to commit about all the mistakes a dunderhead skipper can make and still stay afloat. So, when I preach, you will be hearing the authentic, albeit agonized, voice of experience. In other words, profit by my mistakes. Do as I say, dammit, not as I do!

A third qualification has to do with the last six words of the title of this book, *Without Rocking the Boat Too Much*. I didn't add those words to be cute. They are there because this is to be a treatise with a difference, the difference being an effort to make your excursion as sedate as possible. Milly and I were well beyond 70 years of age when we made our trips to Alaska. I am no longer as spry as I would like to be, and Milly is beset by enough ailments to admit most persons to a rest home. But she said she mostly would be sitting if she spent the summer at home, so why not enjoy it sitting on the boat? Fair enough, but my part, then, had to be to keep things calm. It would be easy to report that I always did, but I am not going to lie to you. A few times, we got into situations that, on hindsight, I know now could have been avoided. Once or twice, Mother Nature fooled me after I had taken all possible precautions. The truth is, you can't make an Alaskan round trip without rocking the boat now and then. That's why the caveat of those last two words in the title, 'Too Much'. I bounced Milly around some in the 1982 trip, but she apparently didn't think it was 'too much'. She was aboard again in 1983.

At any event, here is your author. No expert, for certain. Just a skipper who, after 30 years of coastal navigation between Latitudes 46 and 58 N., believes he knows how one can cruise to Alaska without rocking the boat too much.

Now, how about you, the person for whom I am writing this? Of necessity, I have made some assumptions about you. They are important, but not unusual. They are what I suppose any marine writer assumes about his readers. There is a critical difference, however, between the importance of those assumptions as they might pertain to popular cruising areas such as, say, Puget Sound, and the less traveled waterways of northern British Columbia and Southeastern Alaska. In Puget Sound, one or more other pleasure boats probably are in sight, and rescue units usually are only minutes away. In some areas of a cruise to Alaska, however, help may be a long time arriving. To repeat, then, the assumptions I have made about you are important—critical might be a better word—for a trip to Alaska.

Put it another way. The object of this book is not to guarantee that any Tom, Dick or Jane who happens to have access to something that floats can take off for Alaska at any time. That sort of happy-go-lucky, 'it's no big deal' thing has been done, I suspect, ever since Secretary of State William Henry Seward, in 1867, euchred the Russians out of Alaska for a paltry $7,200,000. Well, despite that, your Uncle Walter is here to say flat out that it *is* important to take seriously the planning of a successful, happy round-trip to the Land of the Midnight Sun.

4

Are You
Ready For Alaska?

The assumptions I am making about a man or woman seriously planning a pleasure boat Inside Passage cruise to Southeast Alaska are listed here as questions to you, the skipper. I am assuming you will answer each question in the affirmative before starting the trip, but if you can't say "Yes" to a question, don't give up your dream. Take enough time to turn that "No" into a "Yes". Rome wasn't built in a day, and taking off for Alaska isn't something you have to do this very minute and second. After all, Milly and I cruised for 30 years and were beyond 70 years of age before we made our dream come true with our first trip there.

The first question will lead us into two subjects that must be covered—you and your boat. Ready? Here we go!

Question No. 1—Could you and your craft experience an hour or so in a three-foot confused sea without you or your boating coming apart at the seams?

Now that's a heck of a question, isn't it? Fact is, the inside waters of northern British Columbia and Southeast Alaska, in the summer, are not usually that lumpy; once in a while, however, they produce confused seas of three feet or more, just as any large waterway occasionally will become roiled.

A confused sea is one where waves are moving from two or more points of the compass at the same time. One cause is a wind shift; that is, the wind may have been blowing for a day or two from, say, the southwest, only to switch to a northerly. For a while, then, both southwesterly and northerly waves will be experienced. Another cause is a wind blowing contrary to the direction of tidal current.

Currents run with strength in some B.C. and Alaskan waters, and winds can blow and shift, but you and I—you afloat using your good common sense, and I in this treatise giving you all the cautions I can think of—are going to do our best to keep that boat of yours level. Chances are we'll succeed. Many folks make the Inside Passage round trip without experiencing any really rough water. But Question No. 1 still should be answered affirmatively. A voyage to Alaska is a long one, and it is only prudent to be prepared for the possibility that, somewhere along the line, you and your boat may experience seas not to your liking.

So ... could your boat take it? The answer does not rest in having me tell you what kind of boat is 'best' for an Alaskan voyage. There is no 'best' boat. Sailboats, planing powerboats, displacement trawlers, shovel-nosed houseboats—they all have their advantages and shortcomings, and they all have been used in successful Alaskan cruises. Shucks, even kayaks have made it. But those kayaks were well found, and they were in the hands of persons who knew not only what their kayaks could do and could not do, but what the persons in them could take. So it comes down to you. Only you should say whether your craft is capable of taking you through an hour or so of the pounding, rolling and pitching that a three-foot confused sea might cause.

But the boat, it's said, can take more than you. How about you? Again, only you know whether you are capable, physically, mentally and emotionally, of hanging on to that tiller or wheel in a difficult sea without collapse or panic. Finally, how about your crew? And *that* brings up a vital point ...

Question No. 2—Will you have aboard at least one other person capable of operating your boat?

If that inquiry tells you that Woodward frowns on anyone trying to make a solo trip to Alaska, you are correct. I do, despite the fact that in the summer of 1983 I met and talked, in Petersburg, to Frank Von Culin, a delightful gentleman from Vashon Island, in Puget Sound, who then was completing a solo roundtrip in the *Bonnie IV,* a charming and efficient 29-foot mini-tug he built himself. Frank had a lot going for him, including the fact that he was a retired commercial tugboat skipper who had made many trips to Alaska.

Even so, I frown on Frank's venture, successful though it ap-

6

parently was and competent though he is. Fact is, I frown on all extended solo cruises anywhere. That's because, in this unfair and troubled life through which all of us move, there are such things as broken legs and arms, heart attacks, strokes, and other incapacitating personal devilments that seem to strike without warning. So, one of my major assumptions is that you will have aboard another person who can operate your ship. Certainly not as well as you do, skipper, but well enough to get the ship and you out of an emergency.

Question No. 3—Have you, and at least one other person who will be making the Alaska trip with you (hereafter, for brevity, let's call that person 'the crew'), taken and passed the advanced piloting course offered either by the United States Power Squadron or the Coast Guard Auxiliary, or, in the alternative, have you and your crew, through experience or whatever other means, acquired the equivalent knowledge taught by those courses?

Please don't fudge on that answer. The lengthy trip to Alaska demands more than just steering ability to hug the shore. Things will get mighty confusing, believe me, unless you (and your crew) can read a chart, plot a course, measure its distance, compensate for current and wind, estimate running time, adjust the true course for both variation and deviation in the compass, and know, at all times, where your ship is.

Question No. 4—Can you and your crew, at the end of the day's run, find the best available protected place, and anchor the ship securely for the night?

You'll do more anchoring than tying to floats, which, in most areas, are mighty few and far between. The answer to No. 4 not only entails the physical details of lowering the anchor correctly, backing down on the rode, and making sure that the anchor is holding. It also involves the ability to read tide tables so that sufficient rode is payed out to provide the correct scope during the highest water that will be experienced while you are at anchor (and they do have *high* tides up north!). Finally, it includes the ability to verify the charted depth of the anchorage with a depth indicator of some kind.

Question No. 5—Can you and your crew operate your ship's VHF radio?

Anybody can turn the off-on switch, but do you have the patience and skill to fine tune your set so that in those areas where reception of official weather broadcasts is poor (there are some), you still may be able to snatch enough key words to give you essential information? It also, of course, means the ability to ask, correctly and intelligibly, for help if you need it.

Question No. 6—Will you be running with another boat that has radar, or will you have radar aboard your own ship and the knowledge to read it?

That puts me on the side of the angels in the debate as to whether you must have radar, either on your ship or a companion vessel. You, of course, are going to avoid running in the fog, in dense rain or at night, but incidents of little or no visibility can develop in midcourse. I've been in thick fog twice on Alaskan voyages; once with radar, and once with only dead reckoning. I'm here to say that there was no comparison; being able to 'see' isolated islands, rocks, critical turning points and other vessels was wonderful.

You don't need Loran or any of the other sophisticated systems now available for offshore navigation and position determination. The Inside Passage route won't take you that far from shore. You don't need an expensive, 24-mile range radar. What you should have—either on your craft or on a ship running with you—is an elementary radar capable of 'seeing' some eight or so miles ahead so that, in poor visibility, you will stay on course and won't bang into immovable or movable objects. That's all, but, in my opinion, you should have that much.

Things To Take

So there you are, saluting smartly, and assuring me that you have a sturdy boat and that you and your crew are ready, willing and able to undertake a cruise to Alaska. Very well, says I. Let's go, says you. Not yet, says I, you haven't assembled the things to take. I have three lists for you.

Things You Must Take

First is the equipment required by law for the size and type of your craft—such things as running lights, horn, flares, fire extinguishers and personal flotation devices. You will be traveling in international waters and, therefore, must comply with the '72 COLREGS (International Regulations for Preventing Collisions at Sea, 1972). I can't help you beyond this point because I don't know the size and type of your boat, and it would be ridiculous to clog this space with a lengthy reprint of the rules for all vessels. They are available for a modest sum at most ship chandleries.

Beyond that, here are seven items you must have:

1.) An accurate compass, either compensated for the magnetic deviation caused by your boat, or accompanied by a deviation table.

2.) Charts, and the tools necessary for plotting courses. To list, now, the more than 50 U.S. and Canadian charts needed (Wow! That many?) would be another waste of space. We'll develop the list as we go along, and there is a complete list in Appendix 1 in the back of this book. As to charting tools, you will want at least a protractor and a pair of dividers.

3.) A depth indicator. A lead line would work, but you'd get tired heaving it. Anyhow, have some contraption to tell you how much water you have under the keel.

4.) A radar reflector. In fog or heavy rain, you need a device that says to other vessels, "Here I am." What's more, the Canadians require one.

5.) A good quality VHF radio. CB won't do.

6.) *Tide Tables, West Coast of North and South America,* published by the U.S. government. You will be skirting coastal shores and must know what the tides are up or down to at all times.

7.) *Tidal Current Tables, Pacific Coast of North America and Asia,* published by the U.S. government. Invaluable for determining precise velocities and direction of current at any time. There will be some narrow passages where you must have that data.

Those are the 'must' items, but here is a footnote on something else. Milly and I have aboard two 'U. Vic. Thermofloat' coats (by Mustang, a Vancouver, B.C. apparel firm). Should we ever have to abandon ship, those coats probably would extend our survival time against hypothermia by at least a couple of hours. We never have used them; *Deo volente,* we never will. End of footnote.

Things You Should Take

1.) Radar. I've already said in the last chapter why I think you should have it.

2.) *Sailing Directions, British Columbia Coast,* published by the Canadian government; two volumes: *South Portion, Juan de Fuca Strait to Cape Caution,* and *North Portion, Cape Caution to Portland Inlet.* They will tell you what charts often can't show—hazards to navigation, current information, wind peculiarities.

3.) *Coast Pilot 8, Pacific Coast Alaska, Dixon Entrance to Cape Spencer,* published by the U.S. government. Ditto the comment above.

4.) *Canadian Tide and Current Tables;* two pamphlets: *Vol. 5, Juan de Fuca and Georgia Strait,* and *Vol. 6, Discovery Passage to Dixon Entrance.* They will give you additional data for B.C. waters not contained in U.S. tables.

5.) A dinghy. At anchor, you'll want to go ashore. You may need it (see No. 7).

6.) A second anchor. I didn't use mine more than once in two trips to Alaska, but was darn glad I had it that time. Besides, it's insurance against catastrophe in the rare event that your main anchor cannot be retrieved.

7. About 200 feet of line in addition to mooring and anchoring lines. You often may want to run a stern line to shore after anchoring. The extra line also will be essential if you are called on to tow a disabled craft (or need a tow).

8.) Spare parts. Go over your boat's motive, electrical and plumbing systems carefully to identify and obtain essential replacement parts. Many communities along the route have well-stocked parts stores, but they may not happen to have the exact size of the 'frignabble' that you may desperately need. There will be a costly delay if a part must be flown to you from Vancouver or Seattle.

9.) Fix-it materials. I always have Marine-Tex, Polyseamseal, and a roll of adhesive duct tape aboard.

Things That Would Be Helpful To Take

1.) *Marine Atlas;* two volumes: *Vol. 1, Olympia to Malcolm Island,* and *Vol. 2, Port Hardy to Skagway.* The best of many marine 'road maps', complete with magnetic course lines, notched for distances, and superimposed on miniature charts (with enlargements of key harbors and passes). Some skippers make the trip with only these two volumes aboard, but they ignore this warning printed on every page: "Not for navigation ... for reference only ... use charts."

2.) *Cruising Beyond Desolation Sound,* by John Chappell. This no-nonsense Canadian's detailed charts and factual comments would be most helpful in finding anchorages between Yuculta Rapids and Cape Caution.

3.) *140 Anchorages, Alert Bay to Juneau,* by the late Dr. McCormick Mehan of Seattle. Out of print, but maybe you can find one to borrow.

4.) Some kind of mechanical gear for hauling the anchor. Be kind to your back.

5.) A boat hook. The tupperware and aluminum things sold these days as boat hooks aren't much, but you can use it to snag things. A sturdy pry it ain't.

6.) CB radio, particularly if you are running with another boat that has one.

7.) Searchlight.

8.) Pocket calculator. Will save much time in navigation calculations.

9.) A 'distance wheel' for charting. Big time saver.

10.) A pelorus for taking bearings or obtaining fixes.

Do I hear you grumbling that it appears you'll have to tow a small barge to accommodate all the things Woodward says to take? OK, I quit. There are my three lists. But hear this: we no longer will be on speaking terms if you don't take all the 'must' items. As to the others, let your conscience and common sense be your guides. Perhaps it boils down to this: how well-prepared do you want to be?

What's that? Do I hear a voice in the background, perhaps a female one, asking "What about food supplies?" Good question. See the next chapter.

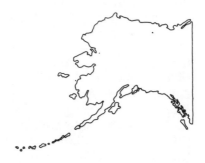

An Overview

Don't cast off for Alaska yet. We have some basic questions to answer such as "What about food supplies?", "What about fuel?", "What kind of clothing should we have?", "How long will it take?", "Shouldn't I bring along a blunderbuss to fend off wild animals and savages?"

The answers are to be found in an overview. Alaska, we all know, is 'up there'; north, that is. The heck it is. If you were to travel true north from Seattle, it wouldn't be long before you'd have to put wheels under your boat and begin to doubt if it could climb all those mountains. A true north course would put you up in Canada's Northwest Territories with Southeast Alaska some 500 miles or more off to the left, or west. Get out an atlas and prove that a cruise to Southeast Alaska must follow a northwesterly course. Note that the line of 122° west longitude passes close to Seattle and that Juneau is at 135°, quite a spell west.

But that is just trivia. How far is it, via the Inside Passage, from Seattle to Juneau? Answer: 879 nautical miles. The southern tip of the Alaska Panhandle (another name for Southeast Alaska) is by no means close to Seattle. There is an enormous amount of Canadian real estate in between. In fact, more than half (about 480 nautical miles) of your trip will be in British Columbia waters. Don't begrudge it. It is gorgeous cruising country and will prove that getting there is half the fun.

Just what is this Inside Passage? Some may not agree, but I think it has its southern beginning off Cape Calvert, the southern extremity of Calvert Island, and ends at Prince Rupert, a distance of some 240 nautical miles. To the west is the wide open Pacific Ocean with its rolling swells and, at times, towering wind-driven waves. But you will be sheltered behind a marvelous mishmash of islands except for the Don Peninsula that forces the big ships (but not you!) briefly out into Milbanke Sound.

Holy moly, only 240 miles of inside waters out of a total of 879?! No. Acutally, an inside passage (forget the capital letters for a moment) begins at Olympia, 'way up at the southern end of Puget Sound, and doesn't quit (save for two unavoidable exceptions) until you reach Cape Spencer, where Southeast Alaska ceases to exist. Let's take it from Olympia. First, there is Puget Sound, an inland waterway sheltered by the Olympic Peninsula. Then there is Whidbey Island, at 50 miles the second longest on the U.S. mainland; it blocks the waves and currents of the Strait of Juan de Fuca. Beyond Whidbey lies the magnificent hulk of Vancouver Island, at 285 miles the largest island on the west coast of North America. Queen Charlotte Sound, an unavoidable open-ocean crossing of some 30 miles, leads to Cape Calvert, start of the (now bring back the capital letters) Inside Passage. North of Prince Rupert, there is another relatively short unavoidable open-ocean crossing called Dixon Entrance. Once that is mastered, you are in the protected inside waters of Southeast Alaska, clear to Skagway, if that is your goal. So, of the 879 miles between Seattle and Juneau, less than 70 are open ocean.

How long will it take? The Seattle-Juneau round-trip can be madᵣ in just eight days if you have a ten-knot ship and run it at top speed for 24 hours a day. And when the skipper has finished, he will be. Finished, and ready for the loony bin.

But you will want to dawdle. You'll want time to snag a king salmon or two, set a few overnight crab and shrimp pots, soak in a hot springs tub, walk a beach or a wooded trail to a nearby lake, inspect some still-standing totems, nudge a glacier, get to know the friendly folks in both British Columbia and Alaska. How much time? Part of the answer lies in the running time required, at your pace, to gobble up those 879 miles. Supposing you cruise at nine knots and are willing to spend about seven hours a day 'moving'. At that rate, which would be tiring for some of us, it will take you about two weeks of steady cruising to get from Seattle to Juneau, or about one month for the round trip. Probably you should allow two or three days of enforced layover for inclement weather. Will three and one-half weeks be enough 'dawdle' time? If it is, then you should set aside two months for the trip. That's not enough to experience all of Southeast Alaska, but you surely could see a great deal in that period.

One thing for certain: please don't go on a tight schedule. The folks who do usually are among those who get into trouble as their time runs out and they force themselves into rough seas or fog banks when they ought to stay at anchor.

What time of year should you go? I've studied accumulated official weather data at five places—Bull Harbor (at the northern end of Vancouver Island and a fairly good source for weather in Queen Charlotte Sound), Ivory Island (about halfway along the Inside Passage), Prince Rupert and Ketchikan (on opposite sides of Dixon Entrance), and Sitka (out on the west coast of Baranof Island). July and August are the warmest months of the year. June and July have the least amount of rain. May and June may be the best midyear months for least amount of fog. July probably is the month with the lowest average wind speeds. Out of all that, I'd recommend June and July with July and August as my second choice. I'd avoid September's increased chance of fog.

To determine the clothing and bedding you'll need, let's examine the weather statistics for July at Petersburg, more or less in the middle of Southeast Alaska. The data: mean daily maximum temperature, 64°; mean daily minimum, 48; mean of the highest, 84; mean of the lowest, 37; mean amount of rain in month, 5.4 inches; mean number of rainy days, 17; prevailing wind, east; percentage of calm condition, 53%. I couldn't find any cloud cover information for Petersburg, but here is Juneau's for July: mean number of days with clear skies; three; with cloudy skies, 23.

To that, add this personal observation for what it's worth. In 1983, we were glad we brought warm shirts and slacks; we experienced considerable rain and cloudy weather that year. But the year before, we had three straight weeks of blazing hot (80°) weather in Southeast Alaska; most of us got dandy tans. The truth is, you never know. It largely depends on whether a ridge of high pressure establishes itself firmly in the North Pacific; if it does, get out the shorts and bikinis; if it doesn't, wear warmer clothing. And always have slickers and rubber boots ready.

Food? Take as many staples as you can mostly because of higher prices up north. If you have a freezer, fill it. But you won't starve. There are well-stocked food stores in at least these places: Nanaimo, Westview (Powell River), Campbell River, Alert Bay, Port Hardy, Bella Bella, Prince Rupert, Ketchikan, Wrangell, Petersburg, Juneau and Sitka. There are many other ports with smaller groceries where the staples may be limited, and the fresh produce and meats are almost sure to be. Check on the food import restrictions currently in force in Canada; one year we had to surrender a bulging sack of lovely U.S. potatoes. And know the federal and provincial holidays currently being observed in British Columbia; it's frustrating to pull up to a float for a shopping expedition only to learn that everything is closed that day.

Booze? Stock it when you can. The grog shops sometimes are far between.

Fuel? There are more gasoline and diesel pumps available than there are groceries. Only skippers of extreme fuel guzzlers should have to do much planning.

That's it, isn't it? Oh, no. What about the blunderbuss for wild animals and restless natives? You shouldn't need it. Besides, Canada is quite firm on its no-firearms rule. The Alaska brown bear is an animal to avoid, particularly a female with cub. The best way is to stay on your boat. If you must go hiking in bear country, take a noisy tin pan and beat it. As for the natives, they are mostly fine people. They like their privacy, particularly in out-of-the-way native villages. If you must call there for fuel or food, do your business and leave. If you want to stay, inquire first to be sure you will be welcome.

16

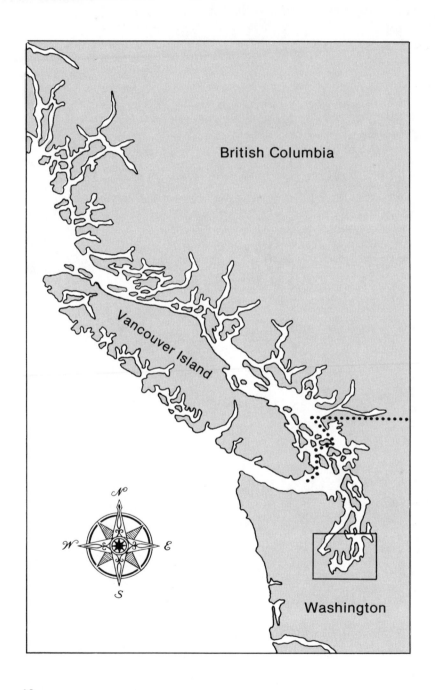

British Columbia

Vancouver Island

Washington

Cast Off!

Cast off! We're on our way to Southeast Alaska!

Henceforth, this treatise will be an effort to assist you, step-by-step, in getting from Here to There. Each chapter will be devoted to a segment of the cruise. Each chapter could be a day's run, but you should not be bound by that idea. A chapter could be only a half day's run if it's your pleasure to barrel along at 12 knots or more, and/or if you intend to keep moving during most of the daylight hours. Or a chapter could be a two-day run in a slower boat, and/or in a craft whose skipper dawdles.

Who cares? Each to his own. The chapters will contain suggestions for overnight moorages along the way; the choice will be yours. There will be a segment or two with a paucity of suitable anchorages, but advance warning will be given so that you won't be caught short.

We know about There; it's the Land of the Midnight Sun. But where is Here? Some skippers may want to gain much time in Alaska by trailering their boats all or most of the way. It's possible. The State of Alaska Division of Marine Transportation operates ferries from Seattle to Ketchikan and other ports in Southeast Alaska. The British Columbia Ferry Corporation maintains service to Prince Rupert from Vancouver and Kelsey Bay on Vancouver Island. If time in Alaska is paramount for you, those ferries—at a cost—would save a lot of it, but you'd be missing much of the 'getting there' fun. Others who want to save some time but who aren't interested in such a lengthy ferry portage will trailer their ships by highway and shorter ferry hops to British Columbia ports north of

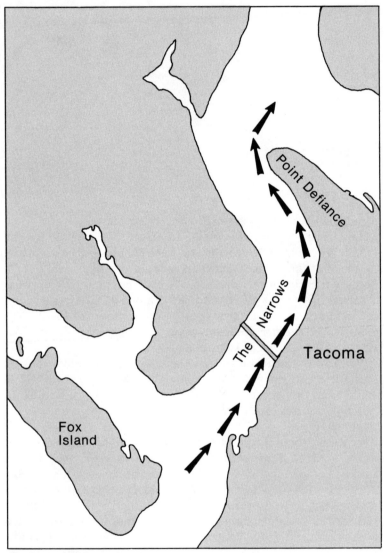

Follow The Arrows
For A "Free" Ebb-Current Ride!

Vancouver such as Nanaimo, Lund, Campbell River, and Port Hardy.

Most skippers who live in Western Washington will be leaving from their home ports anywhere from Olympia at the southern end of Puget Sound to Friday Harbor, close to the Canadian border in the San Juan Islands. Many who live in Eastern Washington, and points east, put their craft in the water at Anacortes close to the San Juans, and save a day or so of Puget Sound cruising. A good number of boat owners from Portland, and points south, trailer their ships to Olympia.

So Here is any place you select. Obviously, I have no choice; I must start writing at Olympia. Join us as we swing by your port of embarkation!

(Olympia to Blake Island)

You should have U.S. Chart 18448 (Puget Sound, Seattle to Olympia; 1:80,000 scale), and some means of determining the directions and times of maximum currents at the Tacoma Narrows.

The scale of this chart is typical of many you will be using all the way to Alaska. The scale results in an easy-to-read marine map for those areas where hazards to navigation are out in the open and easily identified. A nautical mile is a bit less than one inch on the chart. Soundings are in fathoms and depths of ten fathoms or less are shaded in blue.

This area—Olympia to Seattle—is one of the major sections en route to Alaska where saltwater currents will make a major difference; that's why you need to know about the Tacoma Narrows current, on which all the current in the area is based. The currents won't sweep you on the rocks if you don't know ahead of time what they are doing, but you'll really be saving money and considerable time (particularly if yours is a sailboat) if you go with the current instead of bucking it. Note the pass labeled 'The Narrows' just to the west of Tacoma. Through that constriction of about 0.8 of a mile, all the water causing high and low tides in southern Puget Sound surges four times daily, twice into the Sound and twice out, ultimately, to the Pacific Ocean. In The Narrows, for a sweep of at least three miles, the average of the maximum flood (southerly flow) is 3.2 knots and, on occasion, reaches a rip-snorting six knots; the maximum ebbs are about a knot less. You surely are not going to place your northbound boat deliberately in The Narrows at a time of maximum flood; to the contrary, you'll want to hit The Narrows at a time of maximum ebb for a zipping, but safe, 'free' ride.

Your 'free' ride actually will amount to much more than that three-mile dash if you correctly plan your departure from Olympia. On the chart, look at the huggermugger of passes and channels between Olympia and Tacoma. Your course probably will be through Dana, Drayton and Balch Passages. The distance, from Olympia to The Narrows, is about 25 nautical miles. What is your boat's flat-water speed? About eight knots? If it is, then you will get current help of about a knot or more, all the way, if you will plan your Olympia departure between two and three hours before the time of maximum ebb at The Narrows.

The course itself is nothing to fuss about. Follow the well-buoyed channel out of Olympia's Budd Inlet (keep the red buoys and markers on your left because you will be doing the opposite of "returning from sea"). Take Dana Passage in the middle, being sure to give the Itsami Ledge marker a berth of at least 100 yards to starboard. Watch out for sportsfishermen off Johnson Point (if you have time, join them, for it is a salmon hot spot).

After rounding Johnson Point, you have a fork in the road. You could maintain a southeasterly course and swing around Anderson Island's Lyle Point in Nisqually Reach (be sure to keep well off the buoys that mark the suddenly very shallow water of the Nisqually Flats) and then cruise northeasterly, keeping Ketron Island to starboard. It's an interesting excursion that would give you a close look at one of the Pacific Northwest's last remaining great natural estuaries, but it is some three miles longer than a course into Drayton and Balch Passages.

There is nothing to Drayton. Stay in the middle and find the buoy just west of Eagle Island. It marks the beginning of the only 'close encounter' portion of the entire route to The Narrows. Swing easterly and pass the buoy and Eagle Island to starboard and the ferry slip at Bee on McNeil Island to port; for almost a mile you'll have a navigable channel less than 300 yards wide. Then, at a distance off of not less than 100 yards, move along the McNeil Island shore and be glad you are not a guest at the facility there (now a state, not a federal penitentiary). Back there in Drayton Passage, you could have carried on in a northerly direction through

Pitt Passage to reach The Narrows via Carr Inlet and/or Hale Passage, but it is longer and not recommended if this is your first trip; grounding is a definite possibility both in and just north of Pitt Passage.

From McNeil's Hyde Point pass Fox Island, then begin to move over to the Tacoma side of The Narrows. It has the faster ebb current. You should experience considerable current movement, but unless there is a strong north wind blowing against the current, you should not have any difficulty maintaining a course that, in exhilarating fashion, will sweep you up to Point Defiance. Here, you are likely to be in another nest of sportsfishermen.

And here, at Point Defiance, you have another fork in the road. The shorter route (by some four miles) is to continue north into Colvos Passage. An ebb current of a knot or more continues in Colvos until you have reached Blake Island. The longer route, and one without much current, is to turn east at Point Defiance through Dalco Passage and move around Maury Island's Robinson Point into the wide expanse of the steamer lanes in East Passage. One note of caution for Colvos Passage: in season, commercial fishermen may have their nets out; slow down and figure out where the nets are before proceeding; a net tangled in your prop could ruin your whole day.

Just north of Vashon Island, state ferries moving between Fauntleroy Cove (on the Seattle mainland) and Point Southworth will be crossing your course. Unless your craft is moving under only sail, give the ferries the right of way; you are more maneuverable. At any event, once you are a few miles north of Vashon Island you are at the end of Chart 18448. But the chart's mission is accomplished. There, off to your right, is Seattle. At Blake Island, you have come 42 miles from Olympia.

Some notes on likely overnight moorages:

—Squaxin Island, barely eight miles out of Olympia. Find on the chart the two mooring buoys off the eastern side of Squaxin; they indicate a beautiful marine state park with both a float and mooring buoys; beware of depth at the float, however, as it is dusty at low water.

—Filucy Bay, to the west off the northern portion of Drayton Passage. At both ends of this bay there are protected anchorages in two fathoms; commercial moorage at a float may be available at Longbranch.

—Gig Harbor, just west of Point Defiance. The entrance is narrow; slow down, use your depth indicator, and you'll be OK. Several marinas offer float moorage or you can anchor at the west end in two fathoms. Row ashore and treat your crew to dinner out at one of several restaurants.

—Quartermaster Harbor, carved into the southern end of Vashon Island off Dalco Passage. Swing carefully into the bight marked Dockton on the chart. There is a well-appointed county park here.

—Blake Island, two miles north of Vashon Island at the northern end of Colvos Passage. This is the crown jewel of the State of Washington's excellent marine park system. On the island's north side, just around to the west from the Blake Island light, there is a riprap bulkhead that shelters several finger floats. In season, get there as soon as you can in the afternoon; space often is at a premium. But the state also maintains mooring buoys, as indicated on the chart, all around the island; note the wind, if any, and select a buoy that avoids it.

Cast Off!

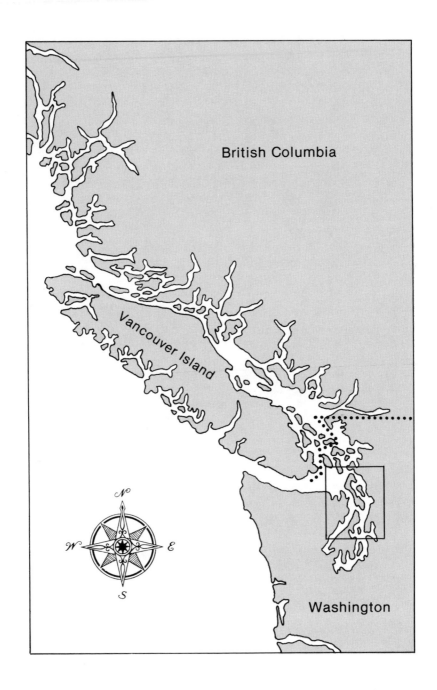

British Columbia

Vancouver Island

Washington

N

W   E

S

Blake Island
To Deception Pass

You should have U.S. Charts 18441 (Admiralty Inlet and Puget Sound to Seattle) and 18421 (Strait of Juan de Fuca to Strait of Georgia); both scales are 1:80,000. A helpful blowup would be U.S. Chart 18427 (Anacortes to Skagit Bay; 1:25,000 scale).

You also should be paying regular attention, several times daily, to the continuous broadcast on the Weather One channel of your VHF radio. Of course, on the run from Olympia to Blake Island, you should not have ignored the weather. For the most part, however, the South Sound is fairly well protected. But Puget Sound is a different ball game north of Blake Island. It both widens (to seven miles in three places) and opens to north-south fetches of 20 miles or more. To be sure, Puget Sound is protected from ocean swells, but it can raise its own hell in strong, sustained winds. The skipper of a deep-keel sailboat might ignore, with good cause, this advice, but I think I would avoid powerboat cruising in Puget Sound if a sustained wind of more than 15 knots is blowing.

For the first 16 miles or so north of Blake Island, your course will take you across vessel traffic separation zones marked in magenta on the chart. Small craft are not required to stay in the lanes, but they should give way to larger commercial ships required to use them. Be particularly wary of tugs; some are mighty powerful and move at a faster clip, even with tows, than you may first imagine.

Also keep an eye out for state ferries. You will be crossing three east-west ferry routes in those first 16 miles. The first one will be south of Restoration Point on Bainbridge Island as ferries linking Seattle and Bremerton follow the island's shore to and from Rich

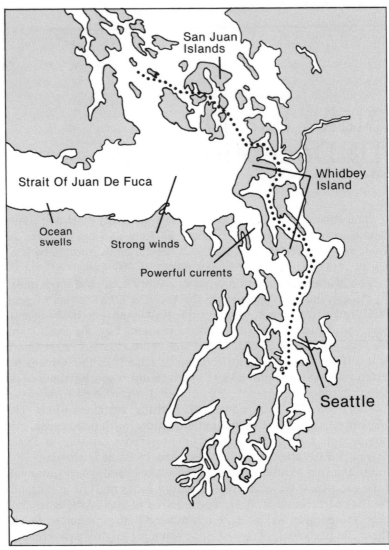

The Sedate Path North

Passage. A couple of miles north, you will cross the path of the Seattle-Bainbridge Island ferries as they enter and leave Eagle Harbor. A dozen miles further north, you will bisect the Edmonds-Kingston (Appletree Cove) route. All these ferries move right along; the ones to Bainbridge Island can travel at 20 knots. Their captains have a lot to do; dodging you (unless you have a sailboat under sail alone) shouldn't be one of their chores; be a good guy or gal and give them the right of way with a clearly indicated course change well in advance. Whistle-tooting shouldn't be necessary, but blow away with the correct passing signal if it will boost your ego; the ferry will respond (I hope).

It might be a good idea to lay out both charts for a moment, with 18421 superimposed over 18441 so as to make a continuing picture. A glance at this larger view should convince you of two things: (1) the calmer path to Alaska is through the protected waters of the San Juan Islands, and (2) the more sedate way to the San Juans is to keep the convoluted hulk of Whidbey Island to port. The charts clearly demonstrate that the sheltered route is in Possession Sound and Saratoga Passage. What the charts do not tell you is additional reason to avoid Admiralty Inlet and the Strait of Juan de Fuca; both are ridden with strong currents, and the Strait is wide open at the west to swells from the Pacific Ocean.

Accordingly, from Blake Island, our course is a 25-mile, almost straight run that keeps Restoration Point to port, West Point and Edwards Point to starboard and the eastern side of Whidbey Island to port. Be wary of sportsfishermen in large numbers off Possession Point, and watch for ferries making the short crossing between Mukilteo and Columbia Beach on Whidbey. Don't crowd the Whidbey shore as there will be innumerable buoys for mooring and crab pots in the way. Continue to follow the Whidbey shore to Sandy Point, then strike out for Camano Island just north of Lowell Point and follow Camano to Rocky Point. In this vicinity, you may wonder about Woodward's non-rocking course if there is a strong westerly wind. You may experience beam seas of enough height to require quartering for comfort, but do not despair. The turbulence will lessen as you cut over to Whidbey's Strawberry Point; if present, the rough water will be caused by the low profile of the isthmus at the western end of Penn Cove admitting wind from the Strait of Juan de Fuca; just be grateful you aren't on the other side!

29

At Rocky Point, you are entering Skagit Bay, a deceptive, shallow body of water if there ever was one. Don't be fooled by that lovely expanse of water; in most places, the bottom is mighty close to the top! Keep the red buoys well to starboard and don't bet on them being in their appointed places. To avoid grounding, use your depth finder as you clear the entrance of the Swinomish Channel; keep Hope Island to starboard, swing around Hoypus Point and there, to the west, is Deception Pass. You have come a bit less than 60 miles from Blake Island.

Likely overnight moorages from Blake Island to Edmonds (just beyond Edwards Point) are plentiful; from Edmonds north they are not so numerous. Beautiful downtown Seattle, oddly enough, has no large commercial facility for mooring pleasure boats. There is a small, free, municipal float at the foot of Washington Street, just south of the Seattle ferry terminal (follow any Seattle-bound ferry), but it is likely to be chuckablock with craft. Seattle's big marina is at Shilshole Bay, a mile or so northeast of West Point; guest moorage is available. Edmonds likewise has a large commercial marina. On the western side of Puget Sound, Eagle Harbor has commercial moorages, or you anchor. You also could anchor in Port Madison's inner harbor at the northern end of Bainbridge Island; the state park just south of Point Monroe is exposed, but there are a few mooring buoys. Kingston has a commercial marina.

North of Edmonds, possible overnight resting places are these:

—Elger Bay, off Camano Island. Anchor, but use your depth finder to keep off the mud flats. No good in a southerly wind.

—Penn Cove, sliced into Whidbey's northern portion. A spot may be available at Coupeville's municipal float, or you can anchor, but it's not the greatest place in strong winds from any direction.

—Oak Harbor, north of Penn Cove. Take care to follow the well-buoyed shallow channel, but at the harbor's eastern end you'll find an excellent, efficiently-operated municipal marina with transient space at floats.

—La Conner, about three miles into the Swinomish Channel. There is a good marina here with transient space, and you won't have to do much backtracking if you intend to use Deception Pass the next day.

—Cornet Bay, around to the south from Hoypus Point. Take

your pick, either float space or tethering to a buoy at a top-flight state park, or find float space at the commercial marina further south in the bay.

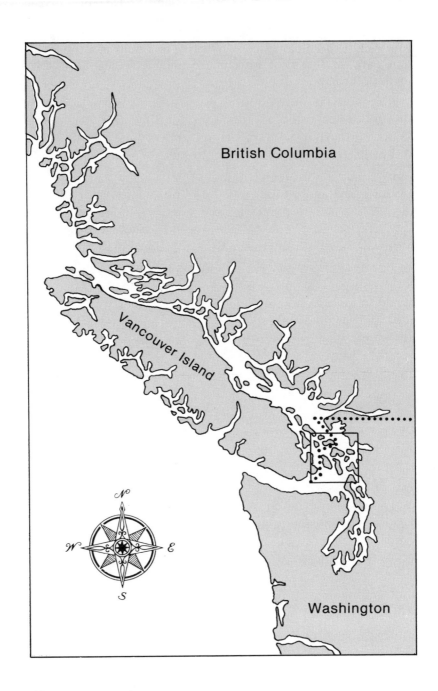

British Columbia

Vancouver Island

Washington

Deception Pass
To Bedwell Harbour

You should have U.S. Chart 18421 (Strait of Juan de Fuca to Strait of Georgia; 1:80,000 scale), and some means of determining what the currents are doing in Deception Pass and Rosario Strait. It would make navigation much easier if you also have U.S. Charts 18427 (Anacortes to Skagit Bay; 1:25,000 scale) and 18434 (San Juan Channel; 1:25,000 scale).

You also should be aware, if you haven't already discovered it, that you are about to lose Weather One on the VHF radio, but the Canadians are ready to rescue you. Punch in Channel 21 and receive the continuous broadcast of nearby Vancouver Radio. It will be featuring forecasts and observations for the Strait of Georgia and Strait of Juan de Fuca, and that's exactly what you should want to hear.

It's a shame, really, what I'm about to do to you. This chapter's only purpose is to suggest ways to get to and through the San Juan Islands, and across the international boundary into Canada. That is akin to rushing through Paradise, for the San Juans are world-famous in themselves as a happy-land cruising area; the Woodwards spent more than a decade of summers in that charming archipelago. But the object of this tome is to get you to Southeast Alaska; if you dawdle in the San Juans—something you possibly can do on the return trip or another summer—you won't have days enough for the Land of the Midnight Sun.

At Cornet Bay, you are one mile and eight miles away from the San Juans. That's not a misprint. I don't mean nine miles. I mean one mile. And eight miles. You must solve that first mile—through

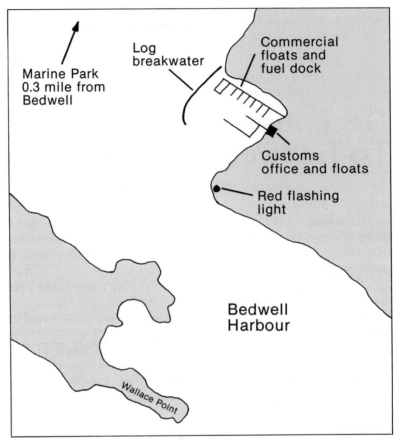

Your First Stop In Canada

Deception Pass—before you tackle the eight-mile crossing of Rosario Strait. One does not necessarily take care of the other. That's because you are facing two different problems.

Deception Pass is one of a very few places where the time of maximum flood, maximum ebb and slack water is affected greatly by geography. It is more of a plug than a pass. Water, struggling to get through, literally 'piles up' on one side or the other, finally rushing through with much turbulence. Its current pattern is unique. Prove it for yourself by checking the Tidal Current Tables for Deception Pass and for nearby Rosario Strait; there is little or no correlation, is there? While you're at it, glance at some of the maximum velocities in Deception Pass; horrendous, aren't they? The average maximum flood is 5.2 knots; the average maximum ebb is 6.6 knots; those are averages, meaning that the current often is much swifter! Therefore, I urge all skippers facing Deception Pass for the first time to make the transit only at the predicted time for slack water. So much for that first mile.

The quickest way to reach the protected waters of the San Juans is to set a true course of about 305° from Deception Pass to reach Lopez Pass, a bit more than seven nautical miles away. But, first, check both the wind and the direction of the current in Rosario Strait. If they are contrary in appreciable strength, you may not wish to go that way. You could be plunging into a confused sea or one whose waves will be on your beam. If you do head for Lopez Pass, here are three tips: (1) If the current in Rosario is at or near its maximum, steer a vector of two or three degrees (to the north if the current is ebbing, to the south otherwise) and you'll accomplish a money and time-saving straighter over-the-bottom course; (2) don't fret about Lopez; it's not another Deception, and (3) after clearing Lopez Pass, be sure to carry on beyond the marker to the southwest of Ram Island before swinging around to a northerly course in Lopez Sound.

To the north of Lopez, there is another crack in the protective ring of the San Juans that you might prefer, Thatcher Pass. It is much wider than Lopez, but carries greater traffic, including state ferries, and is some ten miles away from Deception Pass. If wind is no problem, a course that keeps clear of Williamson Rocks and Dennis Shoal to starboard, and Belle Rock to port, will do it. If there is some northwesterly chop, a little easier ride might be achieved by driving north into Burrows Bay, nipping out along the northern face of Burrows Island, there to reach for Thatcher Pass.

If you don't like the weather in Rosario Strait, but if it isn't really bad enough to keep you from traveling, there still is a third calmer way to reach the San Juans. From Cornet Bay, retrace your course to the marked, dug entrance of Swinomish Channel. Chart 18427 will make it easier to do, but the channel can be taken as it comes and the current is not overpowering. Slow to a no-wake speed while passing La Conner's picturesque waterfront and marinas. After entering Padilla Bay, be positive you stay in the buoyed channel, clear to its absolute end north of the oil depot piers projecting from March Point; believe me, it can get embarassingly dusty just a few feet to either side of that marked channel! Swing around Cap Sante at Anacortes and work through Guemes Channel (it will be slow work, if the current is against you), and continue west to Thatcher Pass. This roundabout path is 14 miles longer, but it is interesting, and will keep you out of Rosario's chop for quite a spell.

At any event, we now are 'inside' the San Juans. Keep Frost Island and Leo Reef to port and swing past both Humphrey and Upright Heads. At this point, there is a fork in the road. The shorter route, and the one that will give you a real feel of the charming nooks and crannies of these islands, is to duck into Harney Channel, squeeze through Pole Pass, navigate Spring Passage and then keep Flattop Island to starboard as you cross Boundary Pass to enter Bedwell Harbour formed by North and South Pender Islands ... in Canada! I would not take that route for the first time, however, if I did not have an adequate chart.

If your only chart is 18421, then, at Upright Head, you should move southwesterly through Upright Channel, then northwesterly in San Juan Channel to a mid-course between Spieden Island's Green Point and Flattop Island and, thence, into Bedwell Harbour.

Find time in Boundary Pass to hoist your Canadian flag in the place of secondary honor on your craft; the place of primary honor, of course, still belongs to your United States flag.

To enter Bedwell, clear Wallace Point on North Pender Island, then move over to the right and gain the quick-flashing red light on South Pender Island. Just beyond this light, you will see some floats tucked into the bight marked South Pender on Chart 18421.

36

Look for the floats reserved for Canadian Customs; there is where you must go first. If you are not boarded immediately by a Customs official, you, and only you, skipper, should go to the Customs office at the upper end of the gangway. Be sure to take your boat registration certificate, and don't fib about the amount of booze and tobacco aboard. Things will go much better if you openly declare what you have. Have in mind about how long it will take you to reach Ketchikan, your next U.S. port; play it safe by asking for a cruising permit that is about one week longer than your estimate.

Via the shortest routes, you have come something less than 35 miles from Deception Pass to Bedwell Harbour.

If you are not going to go straight through the San Juans, the overnight resting places are almost endless. If you must have float space, large marinas are at Friday Harbor and Roche Harbor, both on San Juan Island. Smaller marinas can be found at Rosario, on Orcas Island in East Sound; at Orcas, and at Deer Harbor, also on Orcas Island. Marine state parks abound; among the better ones are those at Jones Island and Stuart Island.

If you are game to try something a little different, find Double Island in West Sound, off Harney Channel. Swing around Double Island's northern end, slow to a crawl, move over to the Orcas Island shore, and set your anchor in about three fathoms for a secure night's anchorage. The great estate just a few yards away once was the retreat of Henry Kaiser, the ship-building and aluminum tycoon. You are entitled to be where you are, but just look, and don't touch. It's private property.

At Bedwell Harbour, take your choice between paying rather handsomely for float space, or moving a bit north to Beaumont Marine Park, a free, provincial (provincial, that is, as in Province of British Columbia) facility with mooring buoys.

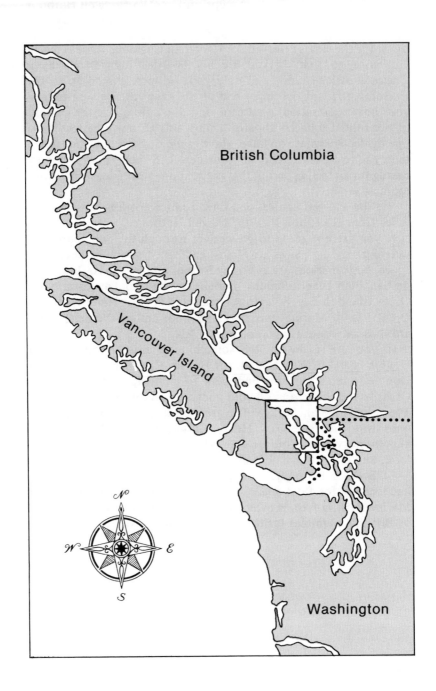

British Columbia

Vancouver Island

Washington

Bedwell
Harbour
To Nanaimo

You should have Canadian Charts L/C3462 (Strait of Juan de Fuca to Strait of Georgia); L/C3463 (Strait of Georgia, Southern Portion); 3443 (Haro Strait, Boundary Pass and Satellite Channel); 3442 (North Pender Island to Thetis Island); and 3443 (Thetis Island to Nanaimo), and you must have a means of determining the time of slack water in Dodd Narrows.

Before leaving Bedwell Harbour, let's pause and consider where we are and why we are taking this route. At Bedwell, we are just barely inside the Gulf Islands. We have just crossed the international boundary from the San Juan Islands. Politically, they are separate. Geographically, they are one archipelago, having been carved prehistorically by the same glacial action. We plunged into the San Juans to keep from rocking the boat too much. We continue on, inside the Gulf Islands, for the same reason. What we now are avoiding is the Strait of Georgia, 20 or more miles wide with an unbroken southeast-northwest fetch of more than 100 miles. When prevailing winds blow with strength over a sustained period along that long stretch of open water, things can be very, very lumpy in the Strait. It is not always that way, of course; Milly and I, several times on pleasant summer days, have made the run between Nanaimo and the San Juans 'outside' in the Strait. But most U.S. pleasure boat skippers, northbound for a Canadian vacation cruise, take the route we are about to follow. The Gulf Islands, like their U.S. cousins, the San Juans, are for leisurely

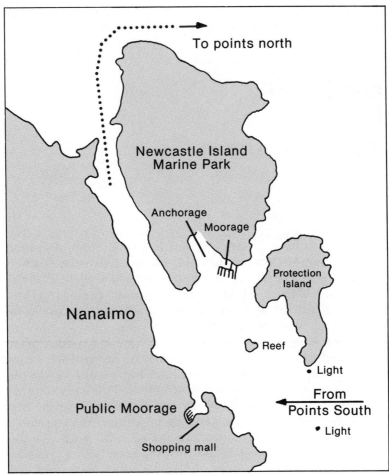

To points north

Newcastle Island
Marine Park

Anchorage

Moorage

Protection
Island

Nanaimo

Reef

Light

Public Moorage

From
Points South

Light

Shopping mall

Nanaimo Made Easy

cruising. So, again, it's a shame what I'm about to do to you. But press on, we must.

At the northern end of the Gulf Islands there are two openings,

Gabriola Pass and Dodd Narrows. It is Dodd we will use to reach Nanaimo. Note that it is not called a pass. Extremely well-named, it is less than 100 yards wide. On the chart, it doesn't look like much, but it begs for your respect. The maximum currents are in the eight to ten-knot range. Slack water, which really never does come to an absolute stand-still rest, lasts about six minutes. That's enough time, for the confines are less than a half-mile in length. The critical thing, particularly for a skipper making his first trip, is to be there about a half-hour before the predicted time of slack water, in case Mother Nature decides not to conform exactly to the prediction. Just south of the pass there is ample room to tread water and size up the situation.

So ... before leaving Bedwell, know what the time of Dodd's slack is and make your departure accordingly. It is about 35 nautical miles from Bedwell to Dodd. If you leave on a rising tide, you probably will have up to a knot of current helping you most of the way. If you leave on a falling tide, you may have that much current against you.

The actual run from Bedwell to Dodd is mostly nothing but a sightseeing trip. Wheel around Wallace Point and skirt the North Pender Island shore. As you cross Swanson Channel, maintain a close watch for large, fast blue and white British Columbia ferries; keep well clear of them, for some produce humongous wakes. Follow Captain Passage to Trincomali Channel, then take Governor Rock on your port hand. Scoot along Wallace Island and the Secretary Islands, all to port, and Hall and Reid Islands to starboard. Stay clear of Danger Reefs and take Round Island to port. Slow down and mosey up to the Narrows on the Mudge Island side. Use your depth finder and favor the Mudge Island side in the Narrows until the exit where you will want to be in midchannel. Cut along the Gabriola Island shore until you can skirt the shallows off Jack Point, then turn west and enter Nanaimo's Harbour. It is shallow, but the channels are well-marked by buoys. You have come some 40 miles from Bedwell.

As you might suspect, the Gulf Islands are full of good overnight resting places. One of the better spots is Montague Harbour on Galiano Island. The harbour's entrance is 13 miles from Bedwell. After emerging from Captain Passage, make a slight course change to the northeast and enter Montague between Julia Island and

Philimore Point; move into and up to the northern end of the harbour to find provincial park mooring buoys and a lovely beach with camping stoves and other facilities in a wooded upland.

Two interesting places somewhat out of your way are Tent Island and Telegraph Harbour. They are reached by keeping Wallace Island to starboard and swinging in Houstoun Passage around Saltspring Island's Southey Point. Tent Island is the tiny one south of Kuper Island; the little bight on Tent's western side is anchorable. Anchorage or float space at commercial moorages can be obtained in Telegraph Harbour, formed by the northern end of Kuper Island and Foster Point on Thetis Island, but beware of those charted rocks near the entrance!

If your calculations didn't quite work out and the current at Dodd Narrows was too much for you, weep not. Turn around and head back some five miles to find, off to the east, Ruxton Passage. Nip through it, then bend around to the north for about a half-mile and, with your depth finder operating and your motive power at a very slow bell, discover the entrance to that almost landlocked harbour near the southern end of De Courcy Island; it's called Pirate's Cove, a dandy anchorage in one or two fathoms.

Nanaimo, itself, is replete with overnight stopping places. A large municipal marina is due west from the harbor's entrance south of Protection Island. The marina is handy to a commodious and well-stocked (with everything except booze) shopping mall (booze is obtained after hiking up a steep hill, but I don't want to hear any complaining; you could give the stuff up, you know). There are other commercial marinas along Newcastle Island Passage, but Milly and I always have favored Newcastle Island Provincial Park, surely the best of all the fine B.C. marine parks. It has both mooring buoys and float space (for which a small charge is made); the entire island is a park, complete with deer and other wild things. A passenger-only ferry links you with beautiful downtown Nanaimo if you must go shopping and don't want to use your own dinghy.

Before we say nighty-night, let's spend a few moments on why we have reached Nanaimo, a former coaling station that now is Vancouver Island's second largest city. In our constant search for protected cruising waters we have found them, but in the finding we have worked our way over to the Vancouver Island side of the

Strait of Georgia. And now, for heaven's sake, we must recross the Strait—sometimes correctly referred to as The Monster—in order to gain the more protected waters along the northern mainland. There are two ways of making that crossing, the way 'everybody' does it, and the Woodward Way. I'll describe both, but first, let's get out Chart L/C3512 and take a good, long look at the problem. Please note that there not only is a great expanse of open water separating Nanaimo from the mainland, but there also are superimposed on the chart two large rectangles labeled 'WG' and 'WF'. These are military exercise areas controlled by the Canadian Department of National Defense; they are used mostly for the testing of torpedoes by a joint task force of the Canadian and United States navies. When they are in use, all other marine traffic is barred. They mean it, and I am here to say that you haven't lived, really, until you have had a large military helicopter, bearing the awesome legend, *Torpedo Range*, hover just above and to one side of your wheelhouse while you frantically and, finally, decide that what the stern-faced pilot wants you to do is to change course drastically and get the heck out of his ocean. To avoid all that, listen to Comox Radio's continuous weather broadcast (Weather One on the VHF); it usually includes warnings of when the torpedo range is scheduled to be active.

So, in my opinion, there are two things wrong with making the 16-mile true north crossing from Nanaimo's Departure Bay to Merry Island: (1) it could be longer if the military is forcing everyone out of Area Whiskey Gulf, the most active of the two rectangles, and (2) a true north course is likely to put one into an uncomfortable beam sea situation, causing some women to take out membership in the Amalgamated Sisterhood of Never Again. But it can be done, and it is done by almost everybody. And at the end of the crossing, there are some charming holes-in-the-wall in which to anchor and lick your wounds, places such as Smuggler Cove, at the north end of Welcome Pass; Secret Cove, about a mile further north, and Pender Harbour. But I have another charming and less-frequented hole-in-the-wall for you, if you would care to follow the Woodward Way. I'll get to it in the next chapter. Nighty-night.

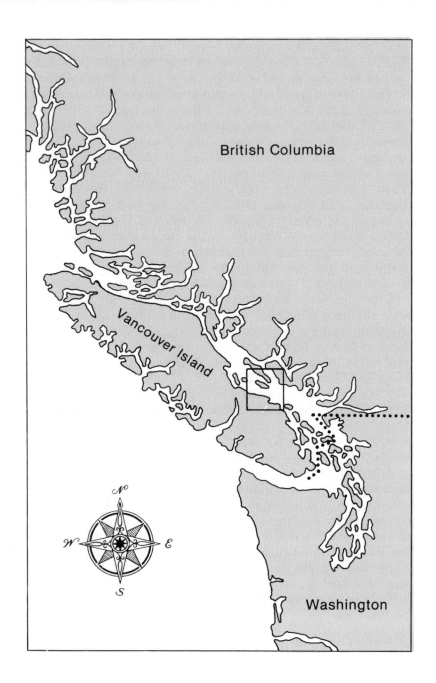

Nanaimo
To Jedediah Island
Or Pender Harbour

You should have Canadian Charts L/C3512 (Strait of Georgia, Central Portion); and L/C3513 (Strait of Georgia, Northern Portion). Alternatively, the new Canadian Chart book 3312 covers the east side of the Strait of Georgia from Lasqueti Island through Desolation Sound.

Regardless of whether you are going to tackle The Monster along with 'everybody', or by following the Woodward Way, the first thing to do is to obtain not only the official weather forecast for the Strait of Georgia, but to pay close heed to reported wind and sea conditions at these three places: Entrance Island (just off the northern end of Gabriola Island); Ballenas Island (a couple of miles off the Vancouver Island shore about a dozen miles northwest of Nanaimo), and Merry Island (close to the mainland shore about 16 miles due north of Nanaimo). The weather condition reports will talk about sea conditions: 'rippled' is a piece of cake; 'choppy' you probably can manage; 'moderate' is a comparative word meaning moderate waves for a freighter, and if you are piloting a freighter, go and have fun, but if your craft is a 35-foot powerboat, stay in port.

If the forecast includes a small craft warning, don't go. Stay in port, have another beer, and listen on the VHF to the agonized complaints of those skippers so foolish as to try The Monster in beam seas of three or more feet.

If you are going with 'everybody', you next must determine if Area Whiskey Gulf is going to be active at the time you will be crossing the Strait; if so, you must make course corrections to go south of the area's perimeter buoys shown on Chart 3577. If you're going the Woodward Way, Area WG is no problem.

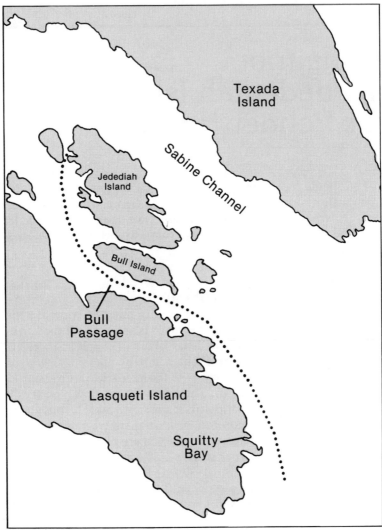

The Hole-In-The-Wall at Jedediah Island

In your pre-crossing planning, you probably will come across a veteran skipper or two; they undoubtedly will tell you that the 'only' time to cross is at the crack of dawn which, in summer, can crack mighty early. There is considerable truth to this advice if the expected wind is a 'good weather' northerly. The summertime northwest wind usually does not rise in the Strait until late morning, and is likely to fade toward early evening. The summertime daylight hours are long and therefore, many pleasant crossings are made in the early evening as well as at dawn's early light. But if the forecasted wind is from the southeast, all bets are off as to the 'best time'. Listen to those weather observations, particularly at Merry and Entrance Islands, then make up your own mind.

If you are going with 'everybody', wheel at a no-wake speed through Newcastle Island Passage, then, paying attention to B.C. ferries and channel buoys, work out of Departure Bay and pass between Five Finger Island and Snake Island on a course that will take you just west of Merry Island, either directly through Area WG or around its southern perimeter buoys. If there is little or no wind, you'll have a lovely trip and will wonder about all this 'monster' talk. However, if a wind of 15 knots or more is blowing, you soon will be rolling in beam seas and will quarter them if the wind is from the southeast. If, however, it is from the northwest, you will be able to do so only if Area WG is not active. Wind from either prevailing direction will be eased as soon as you enter Welcome Pass.

Here's the Woodward Way. After leaving Departure Bay, clear beyond the Horswell Rock buoy by 200 yards, then set a true course of 336° for about 1.5 miles until the 'FIG' buoy is in range with Horswell Bluff. Turn to a course of 294° true for about 5.8 miles until the Maude Island light is abeam to port 200 yards off. A course of 306° true for about 2.5 miles should have the 'IntqkFIG' light in range with Nankivell Point about 400 yards to port. Steer 237° true for about 1.2 miles until you have the north end of Amelia Island abeam to starboard. Run for about 1.8 miles on a course of 314° true until the Cottam Reef buoy makes a range with Cottam Point.

So far, you should have been shielded fairly well from either northwest or southeast swells or chop. Now swing on to a course of 008° true to clear the southern end of Lasqueti Island. If a southeasterly is blowing, you won't be rolled by it until you have cleared Ballenas Island. The distance between Ballenas and Squitty Bay on Lasqueti is six miles. I'd rather be rolled for six miles than for 16 miles, which is the distance between Nanaimo and Merry Island. But you don't need to be rolled by either a northwest or a southeast wind in those six miles; from the Cottam Reef buoy steer a course of 350° true to run north of Sangster Island. That should quarter a northwesterly chop or should put southeasterly waves on your stern. If it doesn't, swing a bit more to port. When you have cleared the northwest end of Sangster, turn to 082° true until you have cleared Point Young.

If your destination is Pender Harbour across Malaspina Strait, steer 029° true to clear Texada Island's Point Upwood, then make for Pender. This will protect you from northwest chop or swells, but if a southeast wind is bothering you too much, forget Pender Harbour and follow me. After clearing Squitty Bay make into Bull Passage. Swing around Bull Island, stay close off the Jedediah Island shore and find the narrow pass between Jedediah and the island lying close to Jedediah's northwestern flank. Halfway through this aperture, turn slowly but sharply east into a dandy hole-in-the-wall anchorage. It has protected the Woodwards at least twice in whistling gales. If there are other craft, you may want to run a stern line to either shore after anchoring. If your stern line has extended length, you should mark it with two or three empty plastic containers to warn other skippers of the line's presence.

At Pender Harbour, you have come about 26 miles from Nanaimo through Area WG and via Welcome Pass, about 34 via the Woodward Way. At Jedediah Island, you have come 25 miles.

A word about the Woodward Way before we note overnight resting places. Most people don't go that way, I suspect, because of all those rocks and islets along the route. There is no question but what more navigation is required both in plotting and steering courses. And it is no good at night or in fog. Purists will say it does, indeed, protrude into Area WG. Picky-picky. It does nip one corner of Area WG off Amelia Island, but only by a teensy-weensy bit and in a part of the area where I'll bet a torpedo never has been fired. Others will say that at Jedediah, one really hasn't completely 'crossed' the Strait. To that, I'd say the crossing certainly has been made; more of that in the next chapter. And the Woodward Way certainly is the calmer way. What's more, it is reversible; on the return trip just use the reciprocal of all those true courses. On the critical turning points I have used ranges; they will be just as good southbound as they were northbound.

As for resting places, I've already called attention to Smuggler Cove and Secret Cove; they are charming places. Further north is Pender Harbour, a rendezvous for yachting people for as long as I can remember; it is chuckablock now with marinas and government docks with floats (note: in British Columbia, there are many 'government docks'; usually their railings are painted a bright red; they are yours to use, sometimes without charge, but space is likely to be at a premium). As for the Woodward Way, you could duck into tiny Squitty Bay and use the government float there ... if there is room. The entire Bull Passage area is notched by likely anchorages; the best one, however, is the one I've indicated at Jedediah Island.

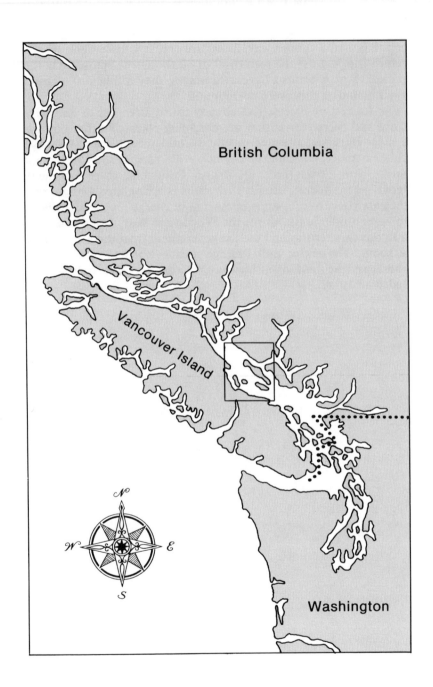

British Columbia

Vancouver Island

Washington

50

Jedediah Island Or Pender Harbour To Desolation Sound

You should have Canadian Charts 3590 (Ballenas Islands to Cape Lazo; 1:77,000 scale); 3591 (Cape Lazo to Discovery Passage; 1:76,400 scale), and 3594 (Discovery Passage, Toba Inlet and Connecting Channels, 1:75,000 scale).

Long straight runs will be the rule from either Jedediah or Pender. From Jedediah, slip along the western side of Texada Island making sure to keep the Monat Islands, a wicked collection of rocks and islets, clear to starboard. At Favada Point, set a course about midway between Vivian Island and Harwood Island, keeping Rebecca Rock to starboard. Carry on with this course until you have cleared and kept well to port the lighted buoy off Mystery Reef, a hideous place of shallows and rocks.

From Pender strike out for Cape Cockburn then continue this course to clear Northeast Point on the east side of Texada Island. Skirt Grief Point, then keep Harwood Island fairly close to port. Just north of Harwood, the folks from Pender will be meeting the folks from Jedediah.

Split the difference between Savary Island's Mace Point and Hurtado Point on the mainland, head for the middle of Thulin Passage, and move along the Malaspina Peninsula shore until you have Sarah Point abeam to starboard. At Sarah, you are at the entrance to Desolation Sound, one of the world's most beautiful and relatively unspoiled summer vacation cruising areas. You have come about 44 miles from either Jedediah Island or Pender Harbour.

If the weather is calm, that's all there is to it, really. However, if

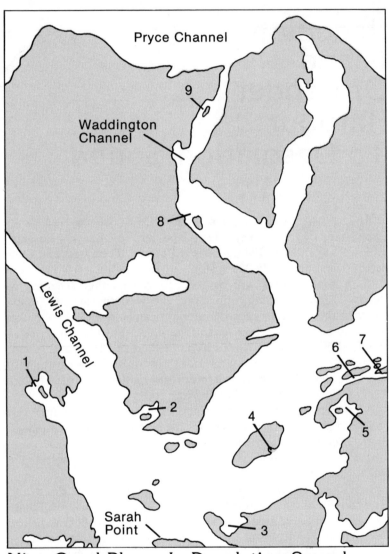

Nine Good Places In Desolation Sound

1-Squirrel Cove
2-Refuge Cove
3-Galley Bay

4-Mink Island
5-Tenedos Bay
6-Prideaux Haven

7-Melanie Cove
8-Allies Island
9-Walsh Cove

a northwest wind is blowing more than 15 knots, the west side of Texada should not be used. It probably will be too choppy. In that event, move out of Jedediah and swing southeast in Sabine Channel, then scoot around Point Upwood into Malaspina Strait to use the eastern side of Texada to buffer you from the wind. Malaspina Strait, however, can be a place of nasty chop if a strong southeast wind is blowing. In that event, those holed up in Pender Harbour might do well to stay there until the wind drops.

If your path north was along the west side of Texada, there simply were no suitable overnight resting places until you cleared Savary Island. There are a few in Malaspina Strait. A delightful charmer is Ballet Bay on the north side of Nelson Island. About eight miles along the Texada shore from Northeast Point is Sturt Bay, not too pretty, what with all the tailings and other accoutrements of a massive lime rock industry, but still a tight anchorage. Two miles north of Grief Point is Westview (Powell River), your last chance at an urban shopping expedition for quite a spell. Crowded moorage (rafting is required) probably can be found in Westview's municipal marina, sheltered by an imposing riprap bulkhead. Transients should use the southern entrance, just south of the ferry slip. But, as at Nanaimo, the grog shop is a long, steep trudge (or taxi ride) up a hill. Are the teetotalers trying to tell us something?

Around the corner from Hurtado Point is Lund's small and crowded marina, shielded by a floating breakwater. Lund may be best loved, however, because it marks the ever-living end of the surfaced highway running north from Vancouver. It is because the highway does, indeed, come to an end that the Desolation Sound area is unspoiled except for some patches of clear-cut logging. For hundreds of miles now, there will be no highway honky-tonks on the mainland north of Lund!

Note the Copeland Islands on the western side of Thulin Passage. They are a provincial marine park; about a mile north of the Copeland Island light, you can work your way (slowly and carefully and with your depthfinder on) into a wooded insular anchorage and, if you select the right place, protection even from the wash of boats using the passage.

Beyond Sarah Point, your only problem will be which anchorage to select. At Sarah, you will have your first awe-inspiring view of the snow-covered, jagged peaks of the British Columbia coastal range to the north and east. When you have recovered slightly from that magical sight of wind-protected sparkling water with charming, wooded islands and peninsulas set against that alpine backdrop, you must listen to your Uncle Walter: dawdle in Desolation Sound if you will, but don't blame me if you run out of time in Southeast Alaska! The way I look at it is this: you probably can come back another year to the delightful cruising areas of the San Juans, the Gulf Islands, Desolation Sound and other equally enticing spots you will discover south of Queen Charlotte Sound. But you may never again mount an expedition to Alaska by crossing Charlotte and pushing on to Prince Rupert and Ketchikan.

So, I'm nagging you to get going. I'll take pity on you, however, by this much. I'll suggest some of the better places to anchor or moor in the Desolation Sound country. Get out Chart 3594.

To find two well-stocked small stores (with booze), keep Kinghorn Island to starboard and move into Lewis Channel. To the west is Squirrel Cove with a government float and store in the southern portion and, to the north through a tiny entrance slot, a landlocked, wooded, blissful, two-fathom anchorage in a mud bottom. To the east in Lewis Channel is Refuge Cove, with a dandy store, fuel dock and considerable float space. They know their English cheeses at Refuge.

Famed anchoring spots in Desolation Sound include Galley Bay on the northwest face of Gifford Peninsula, around to the east from Sarah; the tiny cove on the southeastern face of Mink Island; behind the island in Tenedos Bay; Prideaux Haven and Melanie Cove (get there by crawling along the northern and eastern shores—not the southern—of Eveleigh Island); behind Allies Island (some of us still call it Prussian Island, its pre-World War I name), and at Walsh Cove in Waddington Channel. Oysters abound at most of these places, but be attentive to official 'red tide' warnings and possible boat sewage pollution. Shrimp are a likely catch in Waddington. The salmon fishing isn't much, but it's possible.

Jedediah Island Or Pender Harbour To Desolation Sound

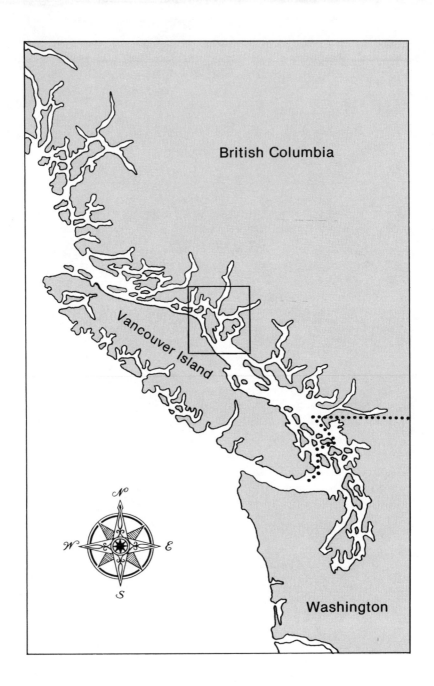

British Columbia

Vancouver Island

Washington

N
W   E
S

Desolation
Sound
To Blind Channel

You should have Canadian Chart book 3312 or 3538 (Desolation Sound and Sutil Channel); 3539 (Discovery Passage); 3541 (Approaches to Toba Inlet); 3543 (Cordero Channel). You must also be able to determine the times of slack water at Yuculta and Dent Rapids.

To reach Alaska via an 'inside' route, you must transit Johnstone Strait or parallel channels. Notice on Chart 3594, in the upper left-hand portion just below East Thurlow Island that a passage of water out to the west is, indeed, labeled Johnstone Strait. That may prompt you to wonder what in the world you are doing in Desolation Sound, 'way to the east. Why didn't Woodward get you over to the west, into Discovery Passage near Campbell River? The answer: because the boat might have rocked too much in the open waters of the Strait of Georgia.

But now that one has come this far north, one can, if it will make him any happier, strike out for Discovery Passage. The way for him to do it is to go west in Baker Passage, keeping off the shoals projecting from both Cortes Island and Quadra Island. If the wind isn't blowing too strong in Sutil Channel, he'll probably reach from Cortes to Quadra without rolling too much, but it is rather open water. As for you and me, we are going north in the protected waters of Lewis Channel and Calm Channel (or in Waddington and Pryce Channels and Raza Passage, if that's a shorter route from your Desolation Sound anchorage).

But right there in Calm Channel, let's drift for a few minutes (put out a salmon line while we talk) and consider the massive challenge that all of us now face, regardless of what route we take.

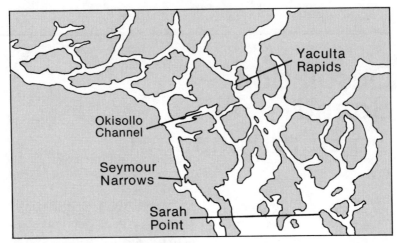

There Is No Escaping
Those Current-Ridden Passes

Current is the problem, tidal current, strong and violent at its maximum strengths. Twice daily, waters from the Pacific Ocean surge (that is a precise word here) from the northern end of Vancouver Island southward through Johnstone Strait and its tributaries, and, twice daily, they race back in the other direction. Where the constrictions are narrow, the current rips and whirls and overfalls (that's a verb I just thought up, but it tells the truth).

The three major places of constriction are: (1) Seymour Narrows, north of Campbell River, (2) Okisollo Channel, cutting between Quadra Island on the south and Sonora and Maurelle Islands on the north, and (3) Cordero Channel along the northeastern face of Sonora Island. There is no escaping them. To get from Here to There, you must go through one of them. I am not trying to frighten you, but I am firm in saying that you must transit any one of them at slack water, and only at slack water. Seymour Narrows has maximum currents that reach 15 knots! Various rock-infested constrictions in Okisollo Channel experience maximums between nine and 12 knots. Dent and Yuculta Rapids, at the eastern end of Cordero Channel, can run at eight to nine knots on the maximum; at time of maximum current, there are huge whirlpools at the northern end of Yuculta Rapids, and dangerous overfalls at Dent Rapids. Got the message, friend? Go only at slack water.

We are aimed for Yuculta and Dent Rapids for several reasons. The current is somewhat less than in the others; the courses are less encumbered by unmarked hazards than in Okisollo, and the route, after clearing the major constrictions, is less exposed and less current-ridden than beyond Seymour.

So ... determine the time of slack water at Yuculta and be in the general vicinity of the Harbott Point light on Stuart Island about one-half hour before the predicted time of slack water. Inspect the rapids and watch other boats which may be fishing in or passing through the rapids. When things look OK to you, go. Even at slack water there will be some turbulence. Push on north until the Gillard Islands light is abeam to port, then turn west through Gillard Passage. Favor the Sonora Island shore; there is plenty of deep water. Keep away from the QkF1R light on the little island marked '190' on Chart 3594. Drive through Dent Rapids. You have made it! You can clear both Yuculta and Dent Rapids on the same slack period if you don't dillydally, especially if you enter Yuculta ten or so minutes prior to slack water there. Where were the overfalls? There shouldn't have been any, if you went through at or near slack. But if you still are curious, the answer is that the overfalls usually occur near the time of maximum current just off the QkFlR light; Milly and I have seen them; they amount to a fall of at least three feet!

There is nothing to the rest of it. Keep Denham Islet to starboard. Steer a mid-channel course between Channel Island and Owen Point, round Godwin Point and pass between Erasmus and Lorte Islands. If Greene Point Rapids, just ahead of you, is at or near maximum current, you may experience some turbulence. Swing around Shell Point and find the extended floats on the east shore of West Thurlow Island marked 'Blind Channel'. There is a small store (with booze and fuel) there. The distance from Sarah Point to Blind Channel via Lewis Channel and Yuculta Rapids is about 40 miles.

This might be the night to treat the crew to a dinner ashore. At any event, in the six or so miles between Blind Channel and Shoal Bay, which is opposite Phillips Arm at the north end of East Thurlow Island, there were, as I write this, three good restaurants. One was ashore from the long government wharf at Shoal Bay, a refuge with considerable float space. Another was Camp Cordero, on a barge moored close to the mainland shore of Cordero Channel just east of Lorte Island; overnight accommodations probably could be obtained here. The third one, a noted place featuring German home cooking and baking, was at Blind Channel.

But if you prefer solitude in a quiet anchorage, try going deep into Bickley Bay, or run about four miles north in Phillips Arm and duck into Fanny Bay. A crab pot, put down in about 20 feet of water near the head of Phillips Arm, just might come up heavy after an hour or so. I don't think I'd leave it unattended overnight; too many sticky fingers around.

Desolation Sound To Blind Channel

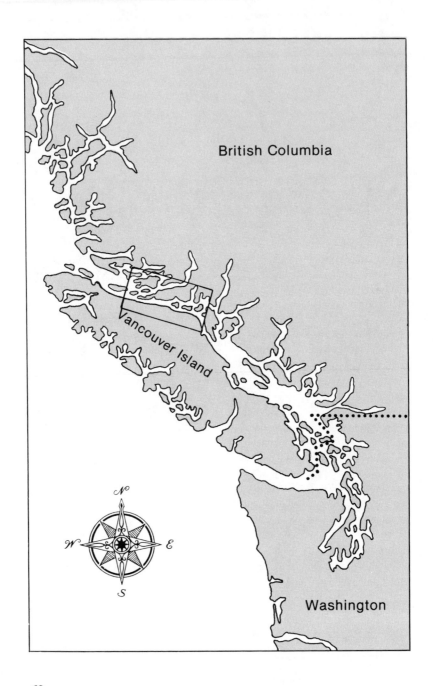

British Columbia

Vancouver Island

Washington

Blind
Channel
To Minstrel Island

You should have Canadian Charts 3544 (Johnstone Strait; Race Passage and Current Passage); 3545 (Johnstone Strait, Port Neville to Robson Bight); and you must be able to determine what the currents are doing in Greene Point, and Whirlpool Rapids, Johnstone Strait, and Chatham Channel.

Preliminarily, it also should be noted that you are about to lose Comox Radio. From now on, for quite a spell, you will depend on Alert Bay Radio, Channel 21, for continuous weather broadcasts.

A glance at the charts will convince you that, at Blind Channel, there are three forks in the road. That first glance also might indicate that the wider, more straightforward route is to follow Mayne Passage out to where it meets Johnstone Strait, then proceed westward in Johnstone. A second path would be to cut through Greene Point Rapids into Cordero and Chancellor Channels and then to go westward in Johnstone Strait. The third route would be Greene Point Rapids, Cordero Channel and Chancellor Channel only to Wellbore Channel, taking Wellbore through Whirlpool Rapids, then following Sunderland Channel to Johnstone Strait.

We will take the last one to avoid as much of Johnstone Strait as we possibly can. Currents are stronger and more dangerous to small craft in Johnstone, particularly when the wind, funneling through the mountains on both sides of the Strait, is in opposition to the direction of the current. The proof is in some excerpts I've taken from *Sailing Directions, British Columbia Coast, South Por-*

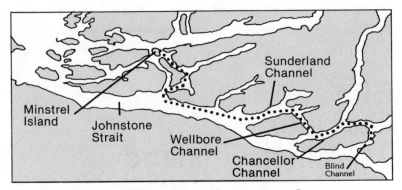

How To Stay Out Of Johnstone Strait As Much As Possible

tion. Please find the referenced areas on your charts as you read these quotes:

Ripple Point ... "At times there is a race, dangerous to small craft, in the vicinity of the point."

Knox Bay ... "Heavy tide rips often form off Needham Point."

Ripple Shoal ... "In the vicinity of Camp Point and Ripple Shoal, the tidal streams attain rates of from three to six knots, with heavy tide rips in the locality at times ... The tidal streams are very strong off Tyee Point, and there are often heavy tide rips in that locality, usually with the flood stream when it is opposed by a strong southeast wind."

Current Passage and Race Passage ... "The tidal streams run strongly through both Current and Race Passages, attaining a rate of nearly six knots at springs; the eddies and swirls are numerous and frequently strong, especially in bad weather when they can become dangerous to small vessels. Over and around Earl Ledge, heavy tide rips and swirls are sometimes formed."

If that doesn't say to the skipper of a small pleasure boat, "Stay to hell out of Johnstone Strait as much as you can," then I'm afraid I don't know how to interpret the English language.

To avoid as much of Johnstone as is possible, we must use both Chancellor and Sunderland Channels. That path, however, poses a problem—the current in both Greene Point Rapids and Whirlpool Rapids. Both reach slack water at about the same time of day. Trouble is, they are about a dozen miles apart. Of the two, Greene probably is the more hazardous to negotiate; it has a turn in it with a couple of bottom-busting islets to be avoided. Whirlpool, more straightforward, does indeed have whirlpools, but it has been my experience that they seem to occur mostly in the wider portions of the channel on both sides of the narrows at Carterer Point; in other words, there may be room in which to be whirled.

There are two ways to solve the problem. The safest simply is to clear Greene at slack and then kill considerable time until Whirlpool is slack again; one could go for a joy ride in Loughborough Inlet or troll for salmon. The other way is to diddle around with the predictions of maximums and slacks at both rapids until you can produce a schedule of transit times to your liking. After all, you no longer are a greenhorn when it comes to taking your ship into current-ridden constrictions; you are beginning to

65

get a feel for what you and your boat can do. I have made six transits through both passes; only once—the first time—did I wait for slack at both. I felt comfortable the other five times when I worked out a transit schedule so that I entered each pass with at least two knots of boat speed in excess of the predicted current. I felt that kept me, not the current, in command.

As to the course itself, there are only a couple of cautionary notes relative to the area covered by Chart 3544. In Chancellor Channel, favor the mainland shore but keep clear of that drying rock just beyond Fittleton Point. In Wellbore Channel take care to give the Midgham Islets and rocks a good berth to starboard. After rounding Althorp Point, the course should keep Seymour Island fairly close on the starboard hand.

When you shift over to Chart 3545, it instantly will become apparent that you finally must transit some of Johnstone Strait. At the western end of Sunderland Channel you simply will run out of parallel channels for awhile. From Gunner Point, you face 13.5 miles of Johnstone until you can wheel around the Broken Islands into Havannah Channel. However, there is some good news; you are joining Johnstone west of all those tide rips and other devilments in the vicinity of Current and Race Passages. In the six transits I have made of those 13.5 miles, five gave me either calm or slightly choppy water. But the northbound run in 1983 was something else again. It was windy in Sunderland Channel, but I didn't think the chop was anything about which to be alarmed. Suddenly, somewhere just beyond McLeod Bay, the big ones—four and five-foot angry white-capped monsters—started to pitch and toss our 46-foot cruiser as though it were a leaf. For about ten frightening minutes, we battled those things until we were able to drive around Tuna Point into Blenkinsop Bay, surely not my idea of a hole-in-the-wall but gratefully received, nonetheless. We got over toward White Bluff and socked the anchor down in about three fathoms with a long scope of chain. We stayed there all day and that night, yawing and rolling somewhat in the remnants of the wild stuff that found its way into the bay. Believe me, we were glad to be there; I would not have wanted to have fought my way the three or so miles to Port Neville, even though Neville undoubtedly would have given us a much calmer anchorage. As I later reconstructed it, the violence was caused by a robust wind slamming into a strong, west-flowing ebb current. Therefore, be warned again, friend; don't venture into Johnstone when vigorous wind and current are in opposition. Do as I say, dammit; not as I do!

When sea conditions warrant, run in Johnstone along the mainland shore until you are well past the Broken Islands, turn true north for a half-mile or so, then get on a course that will carry you clear of Domville Point, the Havannah Islets (to port), and the Bockett Islets (to starboard). When you have Malone Point abeam to port, swing between East Cracroft and Hull Islands until you have gained Round Island.

Here you have a decision to make. About a mile ahead of you is the eastern entrance to Chatham Channel, a waterway so narrow and so set about by rocks that two sets of range markers are provided to guide mariners. The decision you must make is not so much concerned with what may be your first use of range markers, as it is with the strength of the current which can run as strong as seven knots. The current is straightforward and not accompanied by whirlpools or overfalls; it simply can be swift. If you determine that it is too strong for your motive power, then at Round Island you should call it quits for the day and duck into nearby Burial Cove for a snug anchorage in about two fathoms. On the morrow, at a time with less current, you easily can catch up with this chapter's cruising goal of the Minstrel Island area, only about five miles away.

To navigate Chatham Channel, move from Round Island off the East Cracroft Island shore until you find the range markers hidden in the trees at Ray Point. Range markers come in pairs, one placed above and behind the other; the idea is to position your boat, and keep it positioned, so that the two markers visually blend and stay in line with each other. Turn your ship on a westward course; have a member of your crew looking aft and have him/her constantly talking you into an exact course that keeps those two markers in line. You may be alarmed at the masses of kelp close to or actually in your course, but fear not just so long as those range markers are kept in line. About halfway along the channel, you, from your pilothouse, should be able to ascertain and line up the two forward range markers. Excuse your crew from further duty as an aft watch as you steer on those forward markers. Move up fairly close to them; there is deep water; don't cut the corner near the Bowers

Islands. Take the balance of Chatham Channel in the middle and gain the entrance of The Blow Hole and Minstrel Island. You have come 46 miles from Blind Channel.

Good overnight resting places abound in the Minstrel Island area, but en route from Blind Channel there is only one I would recommend. It is Forward Harbour, the entrance to which is about a mile beyond Carterer Point in Wellbore Channel. After you have cleared Robson Point, swing sharply to port. Anchor off the beautiful pebble beach of Douglas Bay; go ashore, tramp the beach and wooded low uplands.

In the Minstrel Island area, there are these:

—Burial Cove, already mentioned.

—Cutter Cove, across Chatham Channel from Minstrel Island. Go deep, use your depthfinder, drop the hook in about two fathoms, and set out a crab pot or two.

—Minstrel Island. Limited float space may be available.

—Lagoon Cove, through The Blow Hole and then south for a tight anchorage or float space. Fuel is available. Favor the Minstrel Island side going through The Blow Hole.

—Potts Lagoon is notched into West Cracroft Island about eight miles into Clio Channel. Keep Negro Rock to port and don't be fooled by Bend Island; slip, very slowly, into Potts Lagoon and anchor in one or two fathoms southeast of the little island marked '35' on the chart. Use your dinghy to put down crab pots just this side of the constriction at the entrance to the inner lagoon. John Chappell calls this "one of the best anchorages on the coast". Milly and I agree.

Blind Channel to Minstrel Island

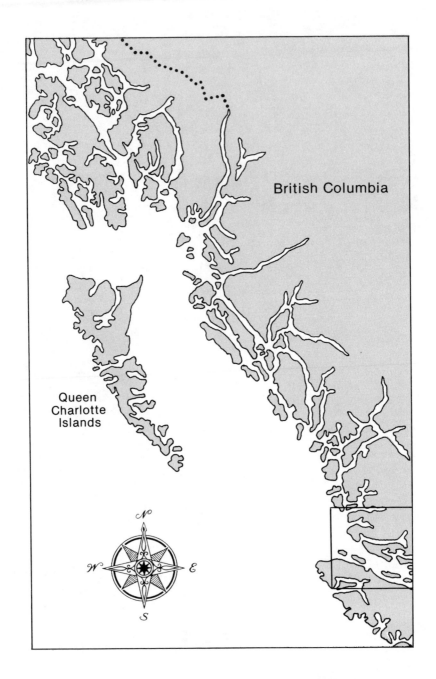

British Columbia

Queen
Charlotte
Islands

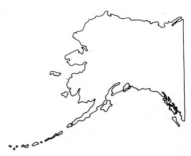

Crossing
Queen Charlotte Sound

Snugly moored as you are somewhere in the Minstrel Island area, you nevertheless should begin to think about your crossing of Queen Charlotte Sound, the first of the two open-ocean challenges that must be endured en route to Southeast Alaska. The crossing still is some 60 miles, or a good day's run away. But, here and now, you must make a decision.

I'm sure we are in complete agreement that we must make the shortest possible actual open-ocean crossing. That means we must find a secure night's anchorage close to the edge of the Sound. There are at least two good ones. They are widely separated, however, and from the Minstrel Island area, are reached by different courses. So now, which one? I'll describe them, you decide.

One is called God's Pocket; it is reached by edging along Vancouver Island on the southern side of Queen Charlotte Strait. The other is Blunden Harbour on the mainland or northern side of the Strait.

From Minstrel Island, the God's Pocket route is some 17 miles shorter, but the Blunden route probably is less exposed to ocean swells by two or three miles. On the crossing from God's Pocket, prevailing swells from the west likely will be on your beam; from Blunden, for at least half of the open-ocean portion, your course line should quarter those same swells for an easier ride. Fog is a distinct possibility on both crossings; the God's Pocket route is relatively free of isolated rocks and islets and can be accomplished in comparative safety by accurate dead reckoning even in fog; the Blunden route, peppered with several offshore hazards, probably

71

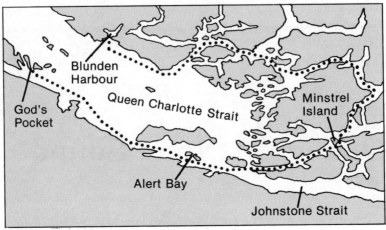

Which Jumping-Off Place?

should not be attempted in fog unless radar is available. The God's Pocket route, at times of salmon runs, can be cluttered with 'wall-to-wall' commercial nets, and is the one used by big, fast cruise ships and other commercial traffic; the Blunden route, which meanders in part through gorgeous cruising country, has comparatively less commercial activity. Finally, but not necessarily least, your last chance at a supermarket for about 150 miles is found only on the God's Pocket route.

I prefer God's Pocket, but many experienced and respected pleasureboat skippers favor Blunden. I'm about to describe both, but first some preliminary thoughts applicable to both routes.

You already may be plotting course lines on your charts; if so, carry on. If not, listen and attend. You now, indeed, are approaching 'fog country'. Both Queen Charlotte Sound and Queen Charlotte Strait, or portions of them, can be socked in with impenetrable fog banks. The easy solution, of course, is to stay put; if it is foggy, wait for it to disperse. Trouble is, it doesn't always work that way. You, at either God's Pocket or Blunden Harbour, may decide that the weather today is clear and take off only to discover halfway across that you suddenly are plunging into one of those blasted fog banks. So what I'm getting around to is this: from now on, at least on legs where you cannot keep a friendly shoreline always in sight, you must have accurate true course lines drawn on the chart, measured and marked for distance as well as heading. These must be drawn before you leave port. And, yes, you must draw them even though you have radar available. Radar is a mechanical thing and can break down. In that event, you must have a backup system of navigation—your dead reckoning course lines. Coupled with those course lines must be sure knowledge of your boat's speed. In other words, you always must know where you are on the chart, what your compass course should be and the estimated time of arrival at the next check point. Up to now, for the most part, you have been able to get by with visual point-to-point navigation. It may be that you will continue to be so fortunate; the number of foggy days in Queen Charlotte Sound and Strait aren't all that numerous. But they do occur, sometimes without warning in mid-crossing. So, friend, please be prepared even if you have a reliable radar. Be ready with dead reckoning.

You have a few other things to do before you plunge across the

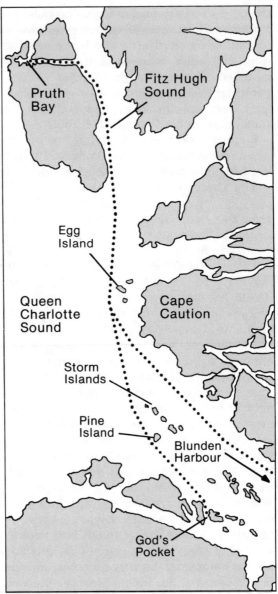

Pruth Bay, Here We Come!

Sound from either God's Pocket or Blunden Harbour. Listen to Alert Bay's continuous weather broadcast, paying particular attention not only to the forecast, but to actual conditions being reported from Bull Harbour and Egg Island. If the wind from any direction either is predicted or reported at more than 15 knots, don't go; wait for better weather. Augment this by looking at the tops of the trees above you; if they are wildly waving, don't go. If there has been a storm in the nearby Pacific Ocean in the last 24 hours, maybe you shouldn't go; there likely will be a residue of heavy swells. Unless you have absolute faith in your radar and/or your ability at dead reckoning, don't go if there is fog.

If the forecast is for northwesterly winds, chances are that they will not rise until late in the morning; a very early start might be a good thing. If the wind is from the southeast, however, it probably will huff around the clock or until it has blown itself out.

There is precious little current information available. About all you can do is determine what the tide is doing. If it is rising, the current, at least in Queen Charlotte Strait, will be flowing east; if the tide is falling the current will be moving to the west; the current velocity may be as much as three knots. Keep this in mind when following your plotted course lines; the current will sweep you, at least in the Strait.

On the run from God's Pocket, you probably won't experience ocean swells until you have cleared Pine Island. On the run from Blunden Harbour, they may not be felt until you have gained the Storm Islands. If the swells are from the west, they will be most pronounced on the 17-mile run from Cape Caution to the southern end of Calvert Island where they will cease (hallelujah!). If a southeast wind is blowing, the damn thing will chase you all the way in Fitz Hugh Sound until you turn the corner at Kwakshua Channel.

In the unlikely event that things become too rough for you in the vicinity of Cape Caution, plot a course to pass between South Iron Rock and Hoop Reef, then follow but hold well off the mainland shore until you can swing into tiny Jones Cove for an anchorage of considerable protection. Our goal on both routes is Pruth Bay at the northern end of Calvert Island, but if the long run to Pruth Bay discourages you, you can slip into Safety Cove some half-dozen miles north of Cape Calvert and cut the day's run short by about 14 miles, but your anchorage won't be nearly as snug as at Pruth Bay.

Crossing Queen Charlotte Sound via God's Pocket

You should have Canadian Charts 3568 (Johnstone Strait, Western Portion); 3569 (Broughton Strait); 3597 (Pultney Point to Egg Island); 3776 (Smith Sound and Approaches); 3727 (Cape Calvert to Goose Island, including Fitz Hugh Sound).

The first portion of the run to God's Pocket lies through The Blow Hole, Clio Channel and Baronet Passage. Preliminarily, it would be wise to ascertain when currents turn in Seymour Narrows, for they turn at approximately the same time in Clio and Baronet. But, be warned! The current in Clio and Baronet runs in exactly the opposite direction from what it does in the nearby parallel water bodies of Knight Inlet and Johnstone Strait. The flood runs out to the west, the ebb surges east! There is nothing catastrophic about this, but you'd better know about it. In Clio, the current may amount to a knot, but it gets stronger as you move west. At Wilson Passage, where Baronet begins, you probably will experience some turbulence and the current may be running at two knots. Around Walden Island, the current, at maximum, can reach five knots. Near Cracroft Point where the currents from Baronet, Blackney Pass and Johnstone Strait collide, there are tide rips and in a strong wind things can get quite bouncy. But it is soon over and, wonder of wonders, you then will discover that the current in Johnstone Strait is moving in the opposite direction from what it was a few minutes ago in Baronet! If all this doesn't confuse you, nothing will.

There are two potential trouble spots in the early going. In Clio, get over to the Klaoitsis Island side to avoid the hazards south of Joliffe Island. In moving past Walden Island, be aware of the charted hazards on the north side and at both ends of the island; with motor at slow bell, depthfinder on, and a careful watch for telltale kelp patches, you should get through OK.

Having gained the wide open spaces of Johnstone Strait, slide along the southern shore of Hanson Island and then set a course that will keep you in the deep water between the shoals off Cormorant Island's Gorden Bluff and Vancouver Island's Nimpkish

River. In this stretch, Johnstone will not be playing tricks on you, the current, which may reach three knots, is straightforward. At Cormorant Island you may wish to put into Alert Bay for a shopping expedition; there is an excellent supermarket and hardware store as well as a grog shop, fuel pumps, and a post office.

If you read the aids to navigation carefully and correctly, you should have no difficulty with Haddington Passage. Make for a spot about 200 yards off Malcolm Island's Pulteney Point. Here, you are entering Queen Charlotte Strait and should have accurate course lines drawn. My marked chart shows that, from Pulteney, I steered 308° true for 12.8 nautical miles. This kept me clear of Round Island, the nearby maze of hazards, and brought me abeam of the Masterman Islands' light. From the light, I steered 296° true for 5.7 miles until I had the eastern end of Duncan Island abeam. I turned to 312° true for 2.6 miles to carry me between the Noble Islets and Hurst Island and into Christie Passage. A northerly course in Christie for not more than a half-mile should bring you abeam of a small bight on the western side of Hurst Island. Turn into the bight and find a small cove with two large government mooring buoys. In fishing season, rafting at the buoys or anchoring may be necessary. It isn't identified as such on the chart, but you are at God's Pocket, a tiny but protected anchorage at the edge of Queen Charlotte Sound. You have come 56 miles from Minstrel Island. (Yes, you could rest overnight at Alert Bay or at Port Hardy—the latter being expensive or crowded, or both—but you'll be adding distance to your crossing of the Sound, 31 miles if you stay at Alert Bay, ten at Port Hardy.)

The course lines to draw from God's Pocket are few, long and simple. It is mostly a matter of keeping clear of the relatively few hazards along the way. You may wish to check your courses with these on my charts: from 0.4 miles off the Scarlett Point light, 324° true for 8.4 nautical miles to a point 400 yards off the Pine Island light; 344° true for 17.0 miles to clear the Storm Islands, to hold more than a mile off Cape Caution, to keep clear of Denny Rock and, finally, to come abeam of the Egg Island light at a distance off of 0.8 miles; 358° true for 21.6 miles to abeam the Addenbroke Island light about one-quarter mile off; 313° true for 4.2 miles to mid-channel in the entrance to Kwakshua Channel; westward for 5.5 miles in Kwakshua to an anchorage in Pruth Bay.

Crossing Queen Charlotte Sound via Blunden Harbour

You should have Canadian Charts 3525 (Tribune Channel); 3576 (Fife Sound and Kingcome Inlet); 3570 (Wells Passage and Adjacent Channels); 3574 (Numas Islands to Harris Island); 3561 (Harbours in Broughton and Queen Charlotte Straits); 3551 (Jeannette Islands to Cape Caution); 3797 (Plans in Vicinity of Queen Charlotte and Fitz Hugh Sounds); as well as 3597, 3776, and 3727.

There are two ways to reach Blunden Harbour from Minstrel Island. The shorter path—by some 20 miles—is to go west to the end of Knight Inlet, then drive northwesterly in Queen Charlotte Strait to Blunden Harbour. It would be a dandy route except for these three reasons: (1) the lower end of Knight Inlet easily can achieve five-foot waves when wind blows adversely to a three-knot current; (2) a dangerous mishmash of mid-channel isolated rocks and shoals, most of them unmarked by aids to navigation, clutters the inlet's western end; and (3) the 27-mile run in Queen Charlotte Strait is wide open to winds from any direction.

The better way, through gorgeous, unspoiled cruising country that may tempt you to make a two-day run of it, is to move north in Chatham Channel to Littleton Point, then to strike out in a northeasterly course to cross Knight Inlet and pass between Gilford and Shewell Islands to gain the easily navigated and protected waters of Tribune Channel. Follow Tribune, which is devoid of mid-channel hazards, around the eastern and northern shores of Gilford Island. Keeping the Burwood Group of islands to port, swing through Penphrase and Sharpe Passages to gain Sutlej Channel. At Sutlej's western end, head for Patrick Passage. But before you reach the passage, you may wish to yield to temptation; off to port is Sullivan Bay, an absolutely delightful place with floats, a store, fuel and other amenities. You have come 42 miles from Minstrel Island, about two-thirds of the distance from Minstrel to Blunden Harbour.

But if you decide to press on, carry through Patrick Passage until you have cleared the Surgeon Islets light, then stay off the mainland (western) shore of Wells Passage until you have the James Point light abeam to starboard about 300 yards off. Here is where you must start drawing accurate and measured course lines, for you are about to move into Queen Charlotte Strait. To avoid the Lewis Rocks, a nasty mess protruding from the mainland for

78

about a mile into Labouchere Passage, plot a southwesterly course that roughly aims for the eastern one-third of the Numas Islands; stay with that course until you are about a mile off the islands, then swing northwesterly on a line that will keep you about a half-mile off the Raynor Group. When abeam of Brandon Rock, get out Chart 3561 and, navigating carefully and with depthfinder on, work your way into Blunden Harbour. The best anchorage probably is in front of the abandoned native village on a line between Byrnes Island and Moore Rock. You have come 66 miles from Minstrel Island, 24 from Sullivan Bay.

The approximate paths for your course lines to Pruth Bay: work out of Blunden and run westerly to a point at least a half-mile south of the Browning Islands; swing northwesterly in Richards Channel between the Millar Group and the Jeannette Islands; when abeam the Jeannette Islands light, turn right to a line that will keep you about one-quarter of a mile off both Wentworth Rock (to port) and Harris Island (to starboard); when abeam Harris Island, turn right again to a line that will keep the Allen Rocks about 0.4 mile off to port and that will bring you abeam the Cape Caution light about one mile off to starboard; turn right once more for a course that will keep Egg Island 0.8 mile off to starboard. The rest of the path to Pruth Bay already has been described in the God's Pocket portion of this chapter.

Incidentally, northeast of Harris Island is the entrance to Allison Harbour, an excellent refuge, but I certainly would not attempt entering it unless I had aboard Canadian Chart 3797 (Plans in Vicinity of Queen Charlotte and Fitz Hugh Sounds), which includes a 1:18,200 scale blow-up of Allison.

At any event, here you are at Pruth Bay (58 miles from God's Pocket; 65 from Blunden Harbour). You have crossed Queen Charlotte Sound, by golly, and have come more than half the distance between Seattle and Juneau!

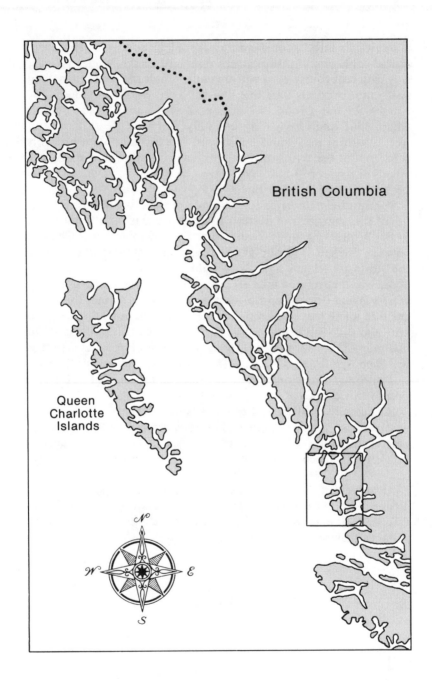

British Columbia

Queen
Charlotte
Islands

Pruth Bay
To Oliver Cove

You should have Canadian Charts 3785 (Namu Harbour to Dryad Point); 3720 (Idol Point to Ocean Falls); 3728 (Milbanke Sound and Approaches); 3710 (Plans in the Vicinity of Laredo and Milbanke Sounds).

From Desolation Sound to Pruth Bay, you have navigated 200 tough miles in narrow, rock-infested and current-ridden channels, and across an expanse of the open ocean with its threats of heavy swells, storm and fog. You have earned an easier time of it. Here it is. Ahead is Prince Rupert, some 220 miles away in the protected waterways of the famous Inside Passage. With a few exceptions, you'll be cruising in hazard-free, relatively wide and fairly straight channels. In only a couple of spots will current be a major factor. The scenery will be pleasant; you'll be surrounded constantly by low-lying islands and peninsulas covered with evergreen trees.

Of course, you will continue to watch the weather and you may have to make some predictions yourself, for there are a few places in the Inside Passage where you probably won't be able to hear a forecast. Remember to be wary of wind and current in opposition. For example, right outside of Pruth Bay, Fitz Hugh Sound can become a choppy mess when a southeast wind slams into a two-knot, south-flowing ebb current.

If there is another problem, it will be finding good resting places at night. You will be passing inlets and harbors galore, but many of them either will be too deep for reasonable anchoring or will be too exposed to wind for calm repose. Under the assumption that you want to press on to Southeast Alaska, I propose to get us to Prince Rupert in four days; that means three nocturnal resting places. I have them, but for those who want to dawdle, I'll continue to suggest alternate anchorages.

There are two ways to leave Pruth Bay. The easier but longer (by three miles) route simply is to go east in Kwakshua Channel, then head north in Fitz Hugh Sound. Otherwise, carefully pick your way among the hazards in the waterway between Calvert and Hecate Islands, and in the narrows between Rattenbury and Hecate Islands to reach Hakai Passage and, thus, Fitz Hugh Sound.

Head for the middle of Fisher Channel keeping the Fog Rocks well to starboard. Swing west into Lama Passage, but don't cut the corner for these two reasons: (1) to avoid that lonely, offshore monster, Walbran Rock, and (2) to stay away from big, wake-throwing cruise ships that are a dime a dozen hereabouts in the summer. Get over to the Denny Island side of Lama and follow it past New Bella Bella. Keep Saunders Island to starboard, but avoid the drying rock off Dryad Point as you turn to port to enter Seaforth Channel. With Rithet Island to starboard, pass midway between the lights on Dall and Regatta Rocks, then set a course that will keep you about 300 yards off Idol Point. From Idol, steer directly for the Robb Point light just off Ivory Island.

Ahead of you is Milbanke Sound and, to the southwest, the wide, wide Pacific Ocean. Cruise ships must go into Milbanke and endure whatever there is to endure out to the west, but not you. Get out Chart 3710 and open it to the plan labeled, 'Channels East of Milbanke Sound'. Maintain your course on Robb Point only until you have cleared Harmston Island, then begin to come right. Pass the red buoy to starboard, keeping the flashing light near Ivory Island to port. Now follow the deep water through Perrin Anchorage, passing Branks Island to port. Ahead is the narrow, but navigable slot of Reid Passage. Favor the Cecilia Island side of the passage until you are about 300 yards away from Carne Rock, a mid-channel menace plainly marked by an aid to navigation. Swing to starboard and pass Carne to port. Move in the passage until you have just cleared Diver Point. Immediately to starboard is your destination, Oliver Cove. On the chart, note the rock in the middle of the cove's entrance. Deeper water is on the north side of the rock; turn slowly into the cove to find a good anchorage in about six fathoms. The cove should protect you during the night from winds of any direction. You have come 53 miles from Pruth Bay.

Some alternate ideas:

—Troup Harbour (I hope that is its name; the chart doesn't say), a winsome place off the beaten path at the north end of Cunningham Island. Instead of turning into Lama Pasage, continue in Fisher Channel until you can get into Johnson Channel. Run to its northern end, then swing west for about a mile beyond Jagers Point. Come sharply to port and work your way deep into the harbor just east of Troup Narrows (when entering, favor the eastern side to avoid rocks). Anchor in about three or four fathoms at the harbor's southern end. To gain Seaforth Channel the next day, use either Return Channel or Troup Passage (if the latter, treat Troup Narrows with great respect and consult the small-scale inset on Chart 3720).

—Fannie Cove, on the south side of Lama Passage, notched into the northern side of Hunter Island. Keep Hogan Rock to starboard, then turn to place Gus Island to port and slip carefully into the cove, anchoring in two or three fathoms.

—Shearwater, in Kliktsoatli Harbour, around to the east from New Bella Bella. A posh resort is here; bring money.

—Kynumpt Harbour, about three miles northwest of Dryad Point. Go deep for a good anchorage in about four fathoms.

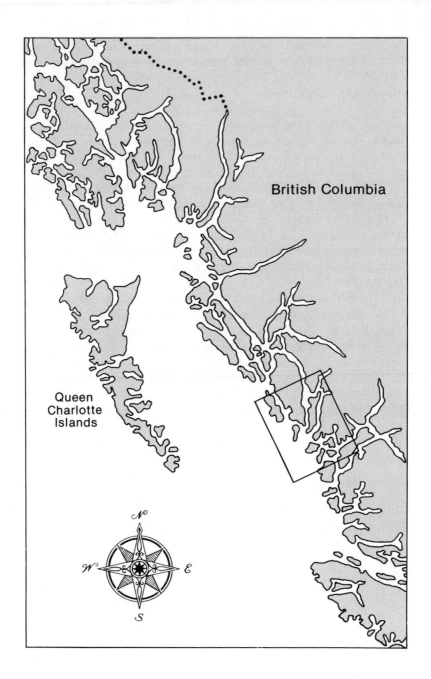

British Columbia

Queen
Charlotte
Islands

Oliver Cove
To Butedale

You should have Canadian Charts 3734 (Jorkins Point to Sarah Island); 3738 (Sarah Island to Swanson Bay); 3739 (Swanson Bay to Work Island).

Most of the tricky stuff in this run is confined to the first three miles. From Oliver Cove, your chore will be to complete the northbound exit of Reid Passage, then move into Mathieson Channel between Lady Douglas and Lake Islands. Perceval Narrows, between Martha Island and the Lizzie Rocks, can be bothersome if the current is running swiftly. Study the tide tables and make the transit closer to either high or low water than to a time of mid-tide; what you should avoid is the five-knot maximum that can boil in Perceval with either ebb (southbound) or flood current.

Move out of Reid Passage until you are beyond Walker Islet, head for the middle of Perceval Narrows so that you stay well south of Lizzie Rocks, then turn to a course that will avoid the shoals off Lake Island. When you have cleared Stapleton Point, run in Mathieson Channel until you have slipped past Arthur Island and can turn west for the five-mile transit of Oscar Passage. As you emerge from Oscar into Finlayson Channel, you may experience swells and/or chop for, at Legace Point, you are not too far away from the ocean. Things will get better though as you head for Klemtu Passage, the slot between Swindle and Cone Islands.

Finlayson Channel, which we are avoiding, not only can be choppy in substantial winds, but, at its northern end, requires a passage through the strong currents of Heikish Narrows. Klemtu Passage, narrow but beautiful, has mild currents. Slow to a no-

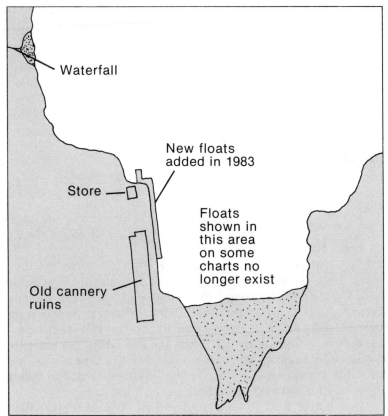

Waterfall

New floats
added in 1983

Store

Floats
shown in
this area
on some
charts no
longer exist

Old cannery
ruins

The Way Butedale REALLY Is

wake speed when passing the exposed floats of the native settlement of Klemtu. Carry past Jane Island and the picturesque red and white lighthouse at Boat Bluff on the southern end of Sarah Island. Enter Tolmie Channel. Off Split Head, at the northern end of Swindle Island, be prepared for some whirlpools as the currents from Tolmie collide with those in Meyers Passage, a convoluted, narrow opening from the ocean. Currents can reach three knots in Tolmie; the flood flows north.

Continue north in Tolmie and swing into Graham Reach at Sarah Head. Favor the Princess Royal Island side of Graham until, just south of Work Island, you catch your first glimpse of the magnificent waterfall at Butedale, your destination for the night. The waterfall, however, is about the only constant remaining from the dim years past when some one drew the Butedale inset for Chart 3739; none of the jim-dandy floats shown at the southern end of the inset exist; the inset depicts what things were like when Butedale was the site of a huge fish cannery, most of which now rots in ruins. But in the summer of 1983, there was a new owner; a gung-ho crew of friendly young people was constructing floats and refurbishing the store. Try to get float space with a north-south axis; the wakes of passing cruise ships rock those moored on an east-west axis. You have completed a long run; you are 64 miles from Oliver Cove.

Alternatives are these:

—Rescue Bay, chiseled out of the northeast corner of Susan Island, just north of Oscar Passage. Go deep into the bay, avoiding the drying rock near the eastern shore, for a comfortable anchorage in about three fathoms. To continue north the next day, either double back to transit Oscar Passage or maneuver through tiny, shallow and rock-strewn Jackson Narrows; try the latter only at high water slack and study the inset on Chart 3734.

—Khutze Inlet, off Graham Reach about six miles south of Butedale. Cruise carefully around the kelp-marked Green Spit, then find the three-fathom spot shown on the chart just east of the spit; a shrimp pot, put down in nearby deep water, might produce a good overnight haul.

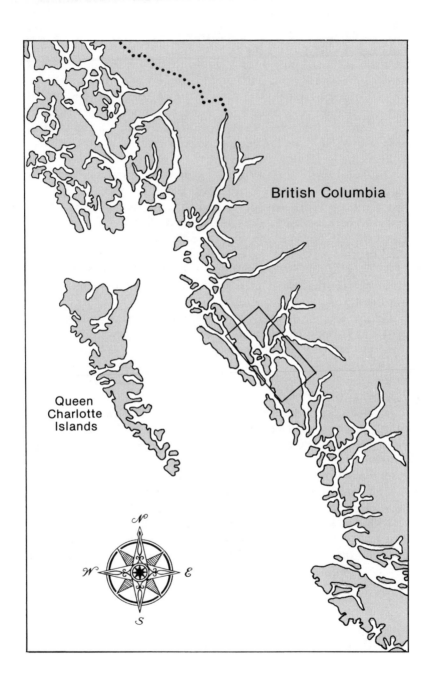

British Columbia

Queen
Charlotte
Islands

Butedale
To Lowe Inlet

You should have Canadian Charts 3740 (Work Island to Point Cummings); 3742 (Otter Passage to McKay Reach); and 3772 (Grenville Channel, Sainty Point to Baker Inlet).

This relatively easy run will take you from one waterfall to another. From Butedale, run northwest to the end of Fraser Reach, swing through McKay Reach, passing Kingcome and Trivett Points fairly close to port, then head for Point Cummings. Cross the sometimes choppy waters of Wright Sound and enter Grenville Channel off Sainty Point.

For 45 miles in a northwesterly direction, Grenville will take you almost to Prince Rupert. But today, after only a run of about 14 miles in Grenville, you will turn off to starboard into Lowe Inlet for one of the better anchorages in the entire trip to Alaska. Enter in mid-channel; there are shoals on both sides of the inlet's opening. Move around Pike Point into Nettle Basin and take your first look at Verney Falls as the Kumowdah River takes its final, frothing plunge to reach salt water. Most skippers will move over to the south side of the basin to anchor.

There is nothing wrong with that, but maybe you'd like to try something that looks difficult, but really is easy and a lot of fun. Steer slowly right for the falls with your depthfinder on and a member of the crew up on the bow, ready to release the anchor at your command. Keep coming for the falls, staying in the river's stream, until the depthfinder tells you that there are about three or four fathoms under your keel. Have the crew let go of the anchor while you take your motive power out of gear. Order enough scope for a three-to-one ratio. The anchor will grab and the river's stream will set it for you. And, for as long as you wish, your ship will stay there with its bow pointed at the falls. You will be lulled to sleep by the lovely gurgle of water moving around your bow as you 'cruise' toward the falls. But you won't move an inch.

(Note: on the southbound return trip, be sure to call at Lowe again. It will be a different scene. In August, there will be less water coming over the falls, but a multitude of good-sized salmon will be flinging themselves over it to reach spawning grounds.)

At any event, you have come 44 miles from Butedale. I know of no good alternate anchorages south of Lowe Inlet.

Butedale To Lowe Inlet

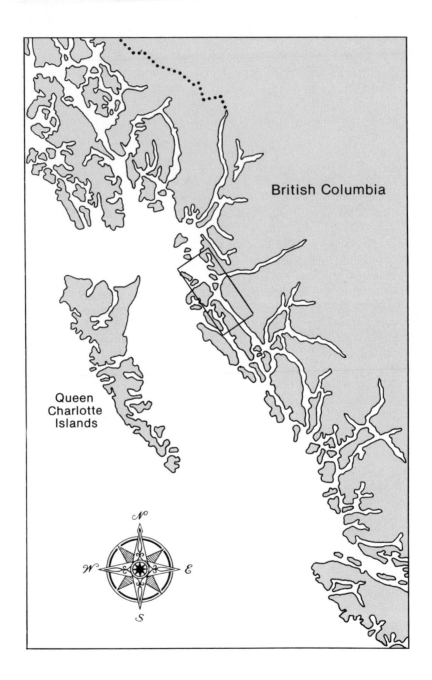

British Columbia

Queen
Charlotte
Islands

92

Lowe Inlet
To Prince Rupert

You should have Canadian Charts 3773 (Grenville Channel, Baker Inlet to Ogden Channel); 3927 (Bonila Island to Edye Passage); 3957 (Approaches to Prince Rupert Harbour); and you should be able to ascertain the time of slack water in Grenville Channel near Evening Point.

To avoid the possibility of thrashing your propeller against a very stubborn, two-knot adverse current, you should understand what the tidal currents are doing in Grenville Channel. The flood current enters both ends of the channel. The two floods usually meet in the vicinity of Evening Point which is about 11 miles north from your anchorage at Lowe Inlet. The ideal thing for you to do, of course, would be to leave Lowe Inlet on a dying, northbound flood, reaching Evening Point at slack, then ride the growing northbound ebb to Chatham Sound. Your U.S. Tidal Current Tables, under the division heading of Hecate Strait and Chatham Sound, give a listing for 'Grenville Channel (narrow portion)'. That's close enough. Figure when the slack before ebb will be. Then leave Lowe Inlet to arrive at Evening Point at about that time. Otherwise, you may be caught struggling against a persistent ebb as you move out of Lowe.

As for navigation, simply go northward in Grenville until you have the Pitt Point light abeam close to port. Steer to keep the Watson Rock light about 200 yards off to starboard, then swing through Arthur Passage, favoring the Kennedy Island side until

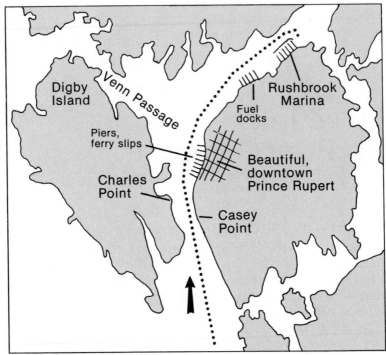

It's Rushbrook For Float Space
At Prince Rupert

you have gained the Herbert Reefs and can strike out for the Hammer Island light, keeping it to starboard about 200 yards off. Pass the Genn Island light about 300 yards to starboard, and turn to a six-mile course that will keep the F1R buoy off Agnew Bank some 100 yards to starboard. Run north for a bit more than three miles to pass the Barrett Rock light by about 100 yards to starboard. You are entering Prince Rupert Harbour; its navigable water is only 0.3 of a mile wide in some places and it is the marine 'Main Street' for a major Canadian port, so keep a sharp eye out for other traffic, big and little.

Follow the Kaien Island (starboard) shore a prudent distance off. Keep chugging right along, past large piers, ferry terminals, fuel docks and beautiful downtown Rupert, its business structures visible above the waterfront, until you reach the place covered by the printed legend on Chart 3957 that reads, 'Floating Bkws'. This is where you want to go. You can enter at either end, but pleasure craft are supposed to congregate in the northern portion. Say a silent prayer for the fishing fleet to be absent and busy at sea, and try to find float space. You may have to raft out. At any event, this is the Rushbrook Marina (public); the fee-collecting office, and the only telephone for taxis, is at the upper end of the gangway, located at the southern end of the marina. Unless you are game for a long, long walk, you probably will want to employ a taxi to go shopping. You have come 57 miles from Lowe Inlet.

Alternate resting places:

—Baker Inlet, about 21 miles north of Lowe Inlet. Beware of strong currents in Watts Narrows; safe transit time would be at slack water. I never have entered Baker Inlet, but the best anchorage appears to be at the head of the inlet.

—Kumealon Inlet, three miles north of Baker Inlet. Favor the north side entering until you have cleared the mess of rocks and islets just south of the entrance to Kumealon Narrows. Swing around that rock pile and aim for the inlet's southern shore until you can anchor in about three fathoms.

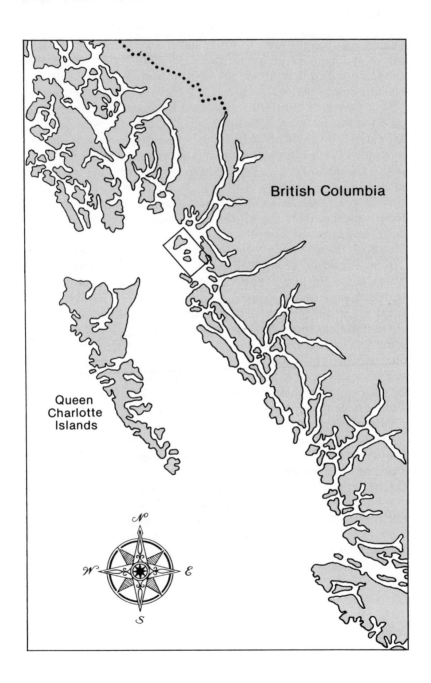

British Columbia

Queen
Charlotte
Islands

Prince Rupert
To Dundas Island

You should have Canadian Charts 3955 (Approaches to Prince Rupert); 3959 (Hudson Bay Passage); and if you decide to leave Prince Rupert via Venn Passage, you should have 3703 (Plans in the vicinity of Prince Rupert, including Venn Passage).

The heading for this chapter isn't misleading—it will describe the path to Dundas Island—but it doesn't tell the whole story because what we really are facing is a crossing of Dixon Entrance. The second of your two required open-ocean challenges, it is much like Queen Charlotte Sound, in that one should try to reach a jumping-off place as close to the actual leap as possible. For Queen Charlotte, it was either God's Pocket or Blunden Harbour. Here, it is Dundas Island, located more or less in the middle of Dixon Entrance at its eastern end. Getting to Dundas in the summer usually isn't difficult; an eight-knot ship can arrive there from Prince Rupert in about four hours. So let's spend some words here and now on the bigger picture, crossing Dixon Entrance.

First, the geography. Dixon Entrance, really an extension of the Pacific Ocean, lies on an east-west axis between Queen Charlotte Island and Southeast Alaska. The gap is about 35 miles, more than ample for westerly and northwesterly winds to raise unimpeded hob. Compounding this is Hecate Strait which joins Dixon near Dundas Island. Hecate lies on a northwest-southeast axis between Queen Charlotte Island and the British Columbia coast. This 30-mile gap opens the door to the nastiness of southerly winds. To complete the potential storm picture of Dixon Entrance, wintertime northeasterly gales called Squamish winds pour into it from Portland Inlet. I should imagine, then, that Dixon Entrance in the winter can be and quite often is an unmitigated maritime hell.

Contrast that, if you will, with this: in the four summertime crossings that I have made of Dixon Entrance, not one of them caused more than a slight discomfort from mild swells and chop. On one of the northbound trips, in 1983, the weather was so nice that we never did pull into Dundas; we just kept right on going. None of that, of course, proves anything except that Woodward was four times lucky. You should respect Dixon Entrance, even in the good weather of summer.

In summer, the prevailing winds in Dixon tend to vary between southwest and northwest. The mean wind speeds are from eight to 12 knots. Fog is a possibility. A flood current, of from two to three knots at maximum, flows to the east off the northern side of Dundas; the ebb, particularly in summer, is not that strong. So much for generalities; now let's move from Prince Rupert to our jumping-off place at Dundas Island.

There are two ways to reach Chatham Sound from the Rushbrook Marina at Prince Rupert. The long way—about eight miles longer— is to follow the route of the deep draft commercial vessels by going south around Digby Island, then swinging to a northwesterly course for Dundas.

The shorter path is to maneuver through all the twists and turns of the narrow and somewhat shallow Venn Passage that winds its confusing way around the north end of Digby Island. You can do it with Chart 3957, but things will be less tense if you have Chart 3955. My chart shows that to reach the eastern end of Venn Passage from Rushbrook Marina I steered a true course of 250° for 2.8 miles. I can't help you any for the next 5.5 miles except to remind you that you are not 'returning from sea' and that you, therefore, must keep all the red aids to navigation to port. I do not think I'd try Venn Passage during maximum current; it can run to three knots. High water slack would be the best time.

After swinging around the northern and western shores of Devastation Island at the western end of Venn Passage, you must take care to stay away from the extensive shoal south of Tugwell Island. Two aids to navigation are there to help you; they mark

Tugwell Reef and the Dawes Rocks. Keep them both to starboard at least 200 yards off.

My charts show that after I had cleared the Dawes Rocks aid, I turned to a true course of 337° for some 16 miles to come abeam of the Green Island light, about 0.4 mile to starboard. A slight course change to 340° true for 3.8 miles took me through Holliday Passage to where I was abeam the Holliday Island light about 200 yards to port. I worked carefully around the shoals off Dundas Island's Whitly Point until I had the Brundige Inlet entrance clearly in sight.

Many skippers who use Brundige Inlet go into the broad bay at its head, but I never have. Instead, I always have turned—very slowly—at Fitch Island, keeping Fitch to port. When I had the south end of Fitch abeam, I turned sharply to port—that's correct, port—and crawled between Fitch and the baring mound labeled '(18)' on the chart. Keeping that mound to starboard, I then went deep into the cove, anchoring in about four fathoms. Off Prospector Point, at the entrance of Brundige Inlet, I figured that I had come 33 miles from Rushbrook Marina.

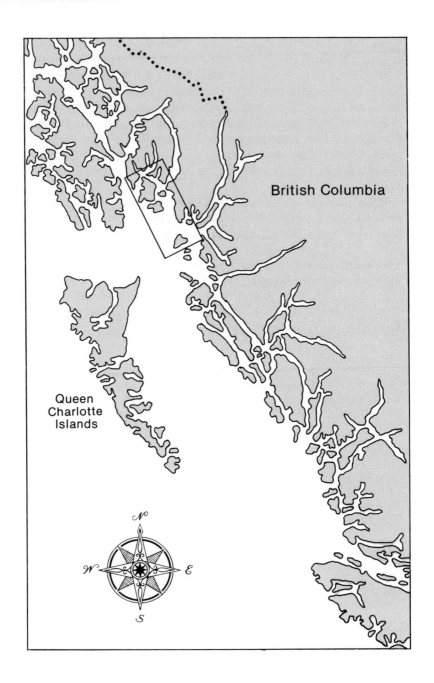

British Columbia

Queen
Charlotte
Islands

Dundas Island To Ketchikan

You should have U.S. Charts 17434 (Revillagigedo Channel; 1:80,000 scale) and 17428 (Revillagigedo Channel, Nichols Passage and Tongass Narrows; 1:40,000 scale).

The usual litany of precautions should be checked before leaving Dundas. Listen to Prince Rupert Radio's continuous weather broadcast; don't go if small craft warnings are in effect; don't go if the wind in Dixon is more than 15 knots; probably you shouldn't go if there had been a fierce storm in Dixon yesterday; go very early in the morning if northwesterly winds are forecast; don't rely on dead reckoning in fog because an area of magnetic disturbance will affect your compass.

After you have worked your way out of Brundige Inlet and have slipped northward between Dundas Island and the Gnarled Islands, you won't have gone more than a couple of miles before you will know whether you belong there. If the going is OK for you and your crew, press on; it probably won't get any worse. If it is too much for you, retreat back to Brundige Inlet; it probably won't get any better.

Your heading beyond the Gnarled Islands should be for a point about one mile off Tree Point, which is north and west of Cape Fox. I advise at least a mile because you are likely to find a nest of gill net fishermen creating an obstacle course along the shore. Between Tree and Foggy Points you will be passing close to an area extending eastward from Duke Island that is labeled 'extreme magnetic distrubance' on some charts and of which the Coast Pilot

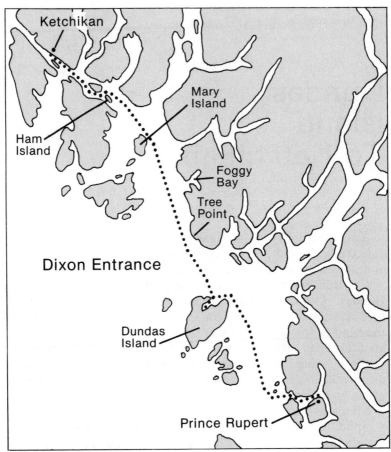

At Last ... Alaska!

says: "The magnetic compass should not be relied upon within the area ..."

From Foggy Point, strike out on a course that will keep you off Mary Island and abeam the Twin Rocks light to port about a half-mile off. Turn to port for a course that will keep the Hog Rocks light to port by about that same half mile.

At this point, whoa, tread water, and wait a minute. Look at your ship's chronometer. What? Don't have one? Oh well, use your watch, then. At Hog Rocks, Ketchikan is 16 miles away. Do you have time to get there, find float space and check in with U.S. Customs? That last item is something you, reentering the United States from a foreign country, must do before anyone aboard your vessel, except the skipper, may leave the ship. I bring this up now because, if you'd rather put off until tomorrow the Customs routine, now is the time to make a course change. Only four miles away is an anchorage at the north end of Ham Island. As long as none goes ashore, you properly can check with Customs tomorrow at Ketchikan. The choice is yours. I'll talk about Ham Island in the alternate anchorages at the end of this chapter.

To reach Ketchikan from Hog Rocks, keep Bold Island fairly close to starboard, give yourself a good clearance of Spire Island Reef to port, then drive midway between Pennock and Revillagigedo Islands and enter Tongass Narrows. When you are off Saxman, call the Ketchikan Port Authority on the VHF; after switching to a working channel, give your ship's name, its length, your location and ask for overnight float space. Hope that some is available, but you might as well understand now—in plain English—that the lack of sufficient transient float space is the bane of visiting most Southeast Alaska ports. Some port authorities are better than others at organizing their available space; Ketchikan does a fairly good job.

At any event, congratulations. You have made it to Southeast Alaska. You have come 54 miles from Dundas Island.

Alternate anchorages:

—Foggy Bay, about eight miles north of Tree Point. I never have stayed there, but the Coast Pilot says that small craft can find 'safe anchorage' in the bay's southeast and east ends.

—Kah Shakes Cove, about eight miles north of Foggy Point. I never have been there, either. The Coast Pilot proclaims it to be a "good anchorage for small craft", but warns that the entrance is impeded with islets and rocks.

—Ham Island, four miles northwest of the Hog Rocks light. Staying well off the Hog Rocks shoals, move past Walker and Lewis Islands and, slowly and carefully, discover the narrow channel separating Annette and Ham Islands. Enter it for about 0.3 mile to find anchorage in about four fathoms. Or, if you prefer, you can find the same cove by going south and then west around the south end of Ham Island, then north in Cascade Inlet. There is a better anchorage behind Pow Island in nearby Hassler Harbor, but you legally can use it only in an emergency because Hassler Harbor is an explosives anchorage area. Wait a minute ... is somebody kidding me? An explosives anchorage behind something called Pow Island?!

Speaking of names, how does Revillagigedo grab you? Quite a mouthful, eh? It could be that the charts err slightly. I'll bet it really should be two words, as in Revilla Gigedo, the name of the viceroy of Mexico at a time when Spanish explorers were poking around in Southeast Alaska.

Dundas Island To Ketchikan

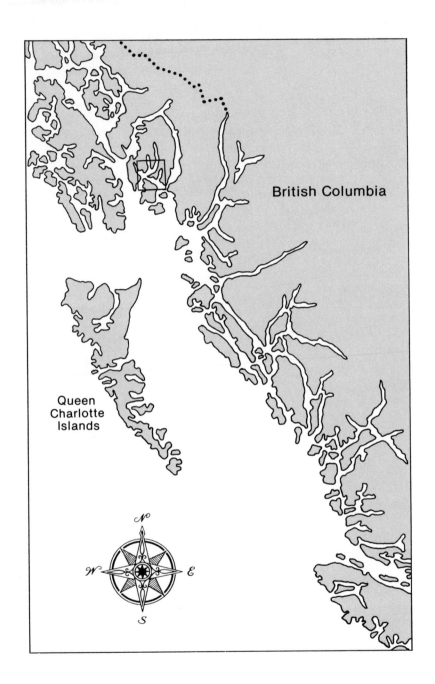

British Columbia

Queen
Charlotte
Islands

106

Another Overview

So here you are in Ketchikan, the gateway to Southeast Alaska. Now where do you go? I know what I must do. I have a commitment to get you to Juneau, and that is what will come next in this book. But I surely have another responsibility. You'll have my head if I don't relax an obligation I steadily have imposed on you. Starting 'way back at the San Juan Islands in Washington state, I have bullied and prodded you to keep going. Don't dawdle, I warned over and over again or you won't have time enough to enjoy the Panhandle. Well, here you are. At last, it's Happy Dawdle Time!

But where, when? Perhaps the answers lie in an overview of Southeast Alaska.

Panhandle is an apt name, but that surely is a mighty big handle. For more than 300 miles, the U.S.-Canada border traces the snowcapped ridges of a coastal range of mountains between Portland Canal on the south and Skagway. That mainland strip is relatively skinny, exceeding 30 miles in only a couple of places, but Southeast Alaska is, roughly, about 120 miles wide. A marvelous conglomeration of huge and small islands provides most of the bulk. Of the six major Southeast Alaska communities, only two— Juneau and Skagway—are on the mainland (and many of the folks who 'live' in Juneau actually reside on nearby Douglas Island). Ketchikan, Wrangell, Petersburg and Sitka all are insular cities. Those islands, buffering the wild storms of the Gulf of Alaska, will enable you to dawdle and cruise without rocking the boat too much.

Where to dawdle? Close at hand, for instance, is an excursion many pleasureboaters take, a circumnavigation in Behm Canal of Revillagigedo Island. A two or three-day venture, it could be done immediately while you are based at Ketchikan or it better might be accomplished with a saving of both mileage and time on the 'going home' run. On our trip to Juneau, we'll make a slight detour to call at Wrangell; there are many charming dawdle coves near Wrangell. We'll also stop at Petersburg where suddenly the scenery will change dramatically to long vistas of jagged, snowcapped mountains spawning awe-inspiring glaciers; you may want to dawdle in or near Petersburg to fish for salmon and/or halibut, entice crab and/or shrimp into your pots, explore iceberg-choked harbors. You'll probably see many more icebergs in the run up Stephens Passage, and may want to explore their calving grounds. You also may want to spend some dawdle time in historic Taku Harbor before pushing on to Alaska's capital.

From Juneau, many possible excursions beckon: Skagway, the famed town of gold rush days 'way up at the ever-living end of long Lynn Canal; Glacier Bay, out through Icy Strait, to inspect closely some of the world's greatest glaciers; Funter Bay, noted for its crab resource; Tenakee Springs, a marvelously independent incorporated village on Chichagof Island, with its hot springs; historic Sitka, Southeast Alaska's most beautiful city out on the Pacific Ocean side of Baranof Island (but reachable via 'inside' waters); the eastern side of Baranof Island with its plunging waterfalls, snow-draped mountains and unbelievable inlets; narrow and intriguing El Capitan Pass, leading you down the western side of Prince of Wales Island to such outpost villages with strange-sounding names as Klawock and Hydaburg.

I doubt if you'll have time to 'do' them all. Milly and I spent two summers in the Panhandle and there still are many fabulous spots we haven't been near. Let's face it: Southeast Alaska is a fascinating place, but its dimensions are frustrating—300 miles long and 120 miles wide.

I'll try to help by this much: I'll lead you to Juneau. Then, in the book's final chapters, I'll try to provide enough detail to smooth the way where navigation is challenging, plus accurate estimates of time necessary for several excursions. It will be up to you to select those places where you will dawdle before heading for home.

Another Overview

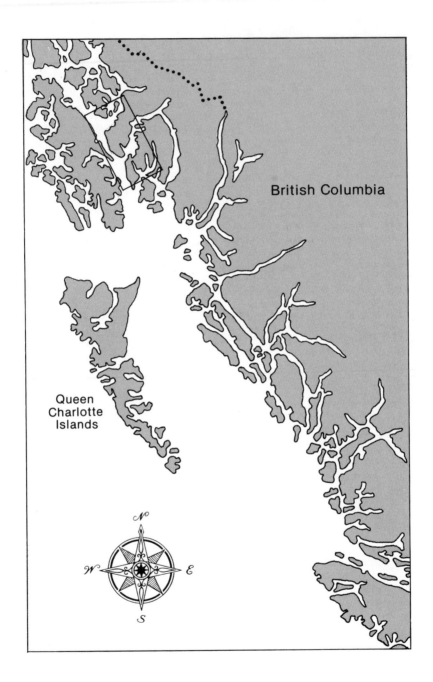

British Columbia

Queen
Charlotte
Islands

110

Ketchikan
To Santa Anna Inlet

You should have U.S. Charts 17428 (Revillagigedo Channel, Nichols Passage and Tongass Narrows; 1:40,000 scale); 17420 (Hecate Strait to Etolin Island; 1:229,376 scale), and 17385 (Ernest Sound—Eastern Passage and Zimovia Strait; 1:80,000 scale). Your entry into some holes-in-the-wall will be easier if you also have Chart 17423 (Harbor Charts—Clarence Strait and Behm Canal, including Myers Chuck and Union Bay, 1:40,000 scale). You also should have a means of determining the direction and strength of the current in Clarence Strait.

In weather that is at least halfway decent, most passages in Southeast Alaska can be made without too much concern. There are a few exceptions, however, and one of them is close at hand as you leave Ketchikan. The snug protection of Tongass Narrows, leading north from Ketchikan, could lull you into trouble unless you first ascertain both the wind and the current situation in nearby Clarence Strait.

The 15-mile-wide mouth of Clarence Strait is agape to the turbulence of both southeast and southwest winds (obviously, northwest winds can blow in the Strait, too). You will join Clarence when you clear the Guard Islands at the northern end of Tongass Narrows; to be sure, that juncture is 45 miles north of Clarence's wide-open mouth, and Clarence's width has shrunk to five miles. But there has been nothing to break the awesome swells and chop that can roll north from the ocean, and that narrowed girth probably does nothing but create a wind funnel, thus intensifying the wind's force. On top of all this potential misery is the blunt fact that despite its ample span, Clarence Strait has very strong tidal currents. The Coast Pilot says that maximum currents of four knots run in Clarence all the way from its mouth to Zarembo Island, a distance of 100 miles!

If I appear to be intense in arguing for your respect of Clarence, I am. I once foolishly was caught off the Cleveland Peninsula in a current vs. wind minor maelstrom for about an hour; whew, the boat rocked ... too much! I want you to avoid that. Listen to the National Weather Service continuous broadcast, paying close heed to wind strength and direction in Clarence Strait; compute the direction and strength of the current at the time you might be off Ship Island. Then decide whether the potential is what you want to endure. Probably I'm being too cautious about Clarence Strait; the truth is, I've had several pleasant passages in it. I know I'm giving you good advice, though, when I urge you not to take it for granted.

As for the courses, there is not too much to fuss about. Pay heed to the aids to navigation in busy, busy Tongass Narrows. Stay a good half-mile off the rock-strewn shores of the Cleveland Peninsula. Swing to starboard around Lemesurier Point, favoring the McHenry Ledge light to avoid the unmarked Lemly Rocks about 400 yards off the point. In Ernest Sound, set a course on Eaton Point for about 13 miles. Keeping tiny Change Island and its attendant rockpile to starboard, work around the southern end of Deer Island and slip into Santa Anna Inlet. Favor the eastern shore of the inlet to its end, where you will be able to anchor securely in about nine fathoms or less. Find an abandoned, rusted boiler on the eastern shore and dunk your crab pots near it. You have come 55 miles from Ketchikan.

There aren't many alternate anchorages that I would recommend. A secure place, however, is Myers Chuck, about 1½ miles south of Lemesurier Point. It has a state-operated float, and there is anchoring room; use Chart 17423 to enter.

Ketchikan To Santa Anna Inlet

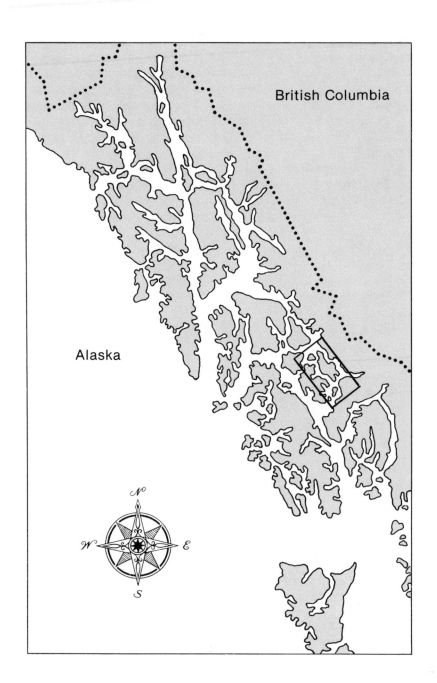

British Columbia

Alaska

Santa Anna Inlet To Wrangell

You should have U.S. Charts 17385 (Ernest Sound—Eastern Passage and Zimovia Strait; 1:80,000 scale) and 17382 (Zarembo Island and Approaches; 1:80,000 scale).

Because Wrangell is on an island, there are two ways to reach it from Santa Anna Inlet. One, six miles longer but requiring less attention to navigation, involves Seward Passage, Bradford Canal, Blake Channel and Eastern Passage. There is one tight spot, The Narrows, 250 yards wide, but with only one hazard plainly marked by a buoy. I never have gone this way, but neither the chart nor the Coast Pilot indicates any major bar to a pleasant and interesting trip through an area apparently devoid of much civilization.

The shorter route is to run out Seward Passage, then swing across the northern end of Deer Island and between Thoms Point and Found Island into Zimovia Strait. The Narrows, a bit more than six miles north of Thoms Point, is a tortuous channel requiring close attention to navigation, but the correct route is well-marked by aids to navigation. Pass the Trap Rock buoy fairly close to port. My chart showed that I then steered 316° true for 1.2 miles. This put buoy C '5' abeam to port about 150 yards off. Then I ran 270° true for about 350 yards until I had the Fl R light ashore beam to starboard. I turned to 223° true and passed midway between the N '10' and C '9' buoys. When I had C '9' abeam to port, I swung to 305° true, a course that kept the Midchannel Rock marker to starboard and cleared the Village Islands to port.

There is nothing to the rest of Zimovia Strait. When you have the Wrangell Institute abeam to starboard, you might call the Wrangell

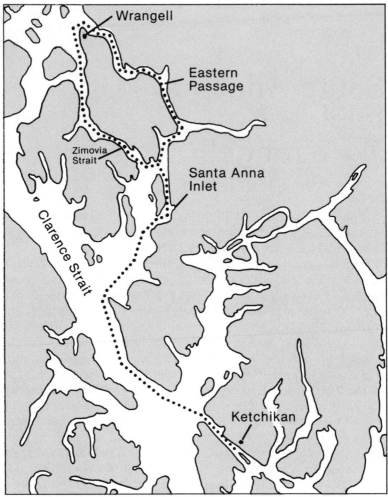

Two Routes To Wrangell

harbormaster on the VHF. He runs a one-man show and is likely to be busy on the floats, but if he is near his radio, he'll answer. It really isn't that important to reach him. There is only one place for a transient ship to go for public float space in Wrangell's small harbor. Swing around the breakwater off Point Shekesti and head southeast in the slot between two long, parallel floats. The float to starboard is reserved for private or commercial uses. The one to port is for transients. It likely will be crowded; you probably will have to raft out. You have come 37 miles (via Zimovia Strait) from Santa Anna Inlet.

There are a few interesting alternate anchorages:

—Anan Bay, in Bradford Canal, about three miles east of Point Warde. It is only a bight, but OK if the wind is from the south. Its attraction is the U.S. Forest Service observatory located a half-mile from the beach; black bears can be watched while they try to snag spawning salmon in Anan Creek.

—Berg Bay, seven miles north from Anan Bay in Blake Channel. Enter on either side of Neptune Island, go deep for anchorage in about five fathoms, and watch for black bear and wolves.

—Anita Bay, about two miles north of the Village Islands in the narrows of Zimovia Strait (use Chart 17382). Go deep for about five miles to the head of the bay for anchorage in about seven fathoms, but have a care for rapid shoaling thereafter.

—Woodpecker Cove, about 15 miles west of Wrangell on Mitkof Island (use Chart 17382). I stayed here once when there was no room at Wrangell. Enter slowly with your depthfinder on. Probably no good if a strong southwesterly is blowing in Sumner Strait.

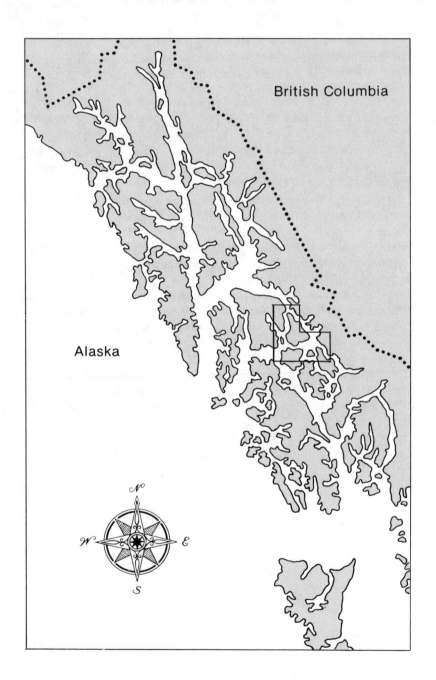

British Columbia

Alaska

Wrangell
To Petersburg

You should have U.S. Charts 17382 (Zarembo Island and Approaches; 1:80,000 scale) and 17375 (Wrangell Narrows; 1:20,000 scale), and you should be able to predict the direction and strength of the current in Wrangell Narrows.

If you can count, you can get to Petersburg.

Once a dangerous, snake-like channel of bewildering shoals and islets, Wrangell Narrows now has more traffic signs than an interstate highway. In a space of 21 miles, there were 63 sequentially numbered aids to navigation in 1983. With a nautical mile taking up more than 3½ inches of space on Chart 17375, it is difficult to imagine how a skipper could stray in good weather from the plainly marked channels. Fog and the gloom of night, of course, could cause catastrophe, but I trust you aren't planning anything like that. And, on the northbound run, not only is 'red right returning' the rule for the aids to navigation, but the lower numbers begin at the southern end of the narrows.

There remain two challenges. One is the possibility that a large and commodious Alaska state ferry or a fast-moving tug with wide tow may wish to contest a particularly skinny portion (100 yards wide) of the navigable stream with your ship. You are more maneuverable and must give way. To avoid such a confrontation, listen on Channel 16 on the VHF for announcements of larger vessels entering either end of the Narrows, keep a sharp lookout both ahead and astern and, at all times, have in mind where the next deep water turnout is.

The other problem is tidal current. The average maximum flood

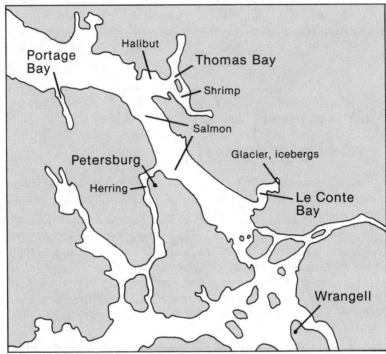

Petersburg Dawdling Places

can reach almost five knots in a couple of places and the average maximum ebb isn't much less. What's more, off your goal of Petersburg, where you must make a sharp turn to starboard in order to gain float space, the maximum flood is 3.7 knots, the maximum ebb is 3.4 knots. You most certainly do not want to be cautiously maneuvering up to a float at Petersburg while an irresistible current is shoving your boat sideways at a merry clip!

Flood currents enter both ends and meet in the vicinity of Green Point, about 12 miles from the southern entrance to the Narrows. This interesting phenomenon provides the solution to the current problem. The safest thing to do is to enter the Narrows at either end during the latter stage of a flood. If this is timed correctly in accordance with the speed of your ship, you should arrive at Green Point just in time to enjoy a beginning ebb flow. The answers are contained in the Current Tables; consult it before tackling Wrangell Narrows.

The southern end of the Narrows is 20 miles from Wrangell. Keep Fivemile Island to port and pass between Vank and Sokolof Islands, taking care to swing north of the Two Tree Island light. Then, keeping Station Island to starboard, work along the Mitkof Island shore until you can turn north at the Point Alexander light and enter the Narrows.

When you are off Scow Bay, call the Petersburg harbormaster on the VHF. If his name still is Jim Stormdahl, you are in luck. Stormdahl, without a doubt, is the best of all Southeast Alaska harbormasters. He works hard at his job, organizes his commercial fleets so that purseseiners are moored together, gillnetters together, and pleasurecraft in another grouping; he knows exactly where the available space is. When you go up to the harbormaster's office to pay your dues, please tell him 'hello' for me. At Petersburg, you have come 41 miles from Wrangell.

I have no alternate anchorages en route to Petersburg to suggest; it is a down-to-earth panhandle city you shouldn't miss; enjoy. If, however, an emergency arises, good anchorage is available at the southern entrance to the Narrows in the bay on Woewodski Island guarded by Deception Point.

There are, however, several dandy dawdling places not too far north of Petersburg. Perhaps it would be a good idea to spend a few words on them now, before we go dashing off to Juneau.

You only need to step on to your float at Petersburg to harvest exciting bounty from the sea. Get a herring jig and a bucket and go to work! Petersburg's harbor is full of flashing, darting herring. Take your haul and run out of the northern end of Wrangell Narrows, turning either right or left, and go a few miles along the shore, then slowly troll for salmon. One hot salmon spot is Frederick Point, about four miles southeast of the Narrows' entrance; another is close to the shore between Beacon Point and Cape Strait (Beacon Point is about seven miles north of the entrance).

To chase a glacier, you'll need U.S. Chart 17360 (Etolin Island to Midway Islands, including Sumner Strait; 1:217,828 scale); use it to enjoy a scenic and exciting day trip to the mouth of the LeConte Glacier. Maybe you'll get there; I didn't. Too many icebergs! From the north entrance of Wrangell Narrows (after spending a few awestruck minutes just looking at the vast expanse of mountains off to the east), I steered 111° true for 12.5 miles. Long before we reached the vicinity of the narrow and shallow pass off Camp Island, we, literally, were dodging icebergs of all sizes and shapes. Let it be said for Woodward that he did make it, nervously, through that pass. But LeConte Bay was too choked with icebergs for prudent navigation. Maybe you'll be luckier, but don't plan on anchoring in LeConte Bay; it is too deep.

For some peaceful and beautiful overnight anchorages near Petersburg, you'll want U.S. Chart 17367 (Thomas, Farragut and Portage Bays; 1:40,000 scale). The narrow channel into Thomas Bay is about ten miles north of the northern entrance to Wrangell Narrows. Before entering, you must locate all three of the buoys shown on Chart 17367; there is foul ground close at hand on both sides of the channel. Push into Thomas Bay on a course that will keep you clear of the north end of Ruth Island. Take time to enjoy the grandeur of the receding Baird Glacier, then swing along the eastern side of Ruth Island to anchor in either of the two bays that indent that side. Halibut are caught in the entrance to Thomas Bay. I'm told that salmon abound off Spray Island. We caught shrimp in the Ruth Island bay marked 'log float'.

Portage Bay, seven miles west of Cape Strait, is likewise somewhat difficult to enter, but it is peaceful after it is gained. The safest bet would be to enter at high water slack. About a mile north of well-named Stop Island, stop. Put the anchor down in about four fathoms for a secure overnight stay.

If you guess from all this chatter that I am very partial to Petersburg and its environs, you are correct. Petersburg, with its no-nonsense yet friendly people, and its gorgeous scenery is to me the epitome of Southeast Alaska.

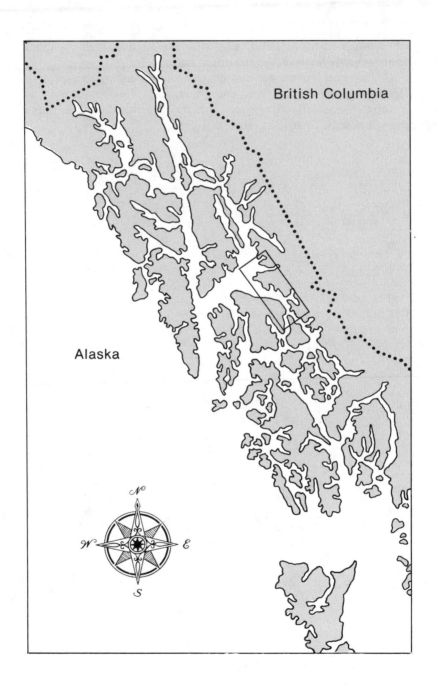

British Columbia

Alaska

Petersburg
To Entrance Island

You should have U.S. Charts 17360 (Etolin Island to Midway Islands; 1:217,828 scale) and 17363 (Pybus, Hobart and Windham Bays; 1:40,000 scale).

I suppose that if you wanted to make the effort, you could cruise from Petersburg to Juneau in one day. The distance is a bit more than 100 miles, and if you get going very, very early in the morning ...

No? Sensible decision, my friend, for two reasons: (1) 'very, very early in the morning' is no time to do *anything* except stay in the sack, and (2) some of the best dawdling spots in all the Panhandle are between Petersburg and Juneau. One of them is our destination in this chapter, Entrance Island, a charming jot in the mouth of Hobart Bay.

Our passage will be in Frederick Sound and Stephens Passage, the channel that ultimately will take us within sight of Juneau. Frederick Sound is a bow-shaped waterway that links Chatham Strait, off to the west, with Sumner Strait near Wrangell. We will be using only a small portion of the eastern section of Frederick Sound for a 30-mile run from Petersburg to Cape Fanshaw and Stephens Passage. Frederick Sound's weather usually is benign in the summer, and there are no offshore hazards after the Sukoi Islets are cleared. They are about four miles north of the entrance to Wrangell Narrows and there is plenty of room to pass between them and the Kupreanof Island shore. After clearing the Cape Strait light, set a course diagonally across Frederick Sound to pass the Cape Fanshaw light about one-half mile off to starboard.

Stephens Passage is a different ball game. It has a 65-mile north-south fetch that should be respected if the wind is more than a summer breeze. What really should command the skipper's attention are mid-channel obstacles, both fixed and floating. The worse of the fixed are in front of you as you round Cape Fanshaw. A bit more than a mile away are the Storm Islands, a mile-long nasty collection of islets, reefs and rocks. Bird Rock light almost guards the southern end of this rock pile; I say 'almost' because an underwater ledge extends for 300 yards west-southwest from the light. If it had not been for an alert grandson who saw a patch of kelp in time, I very well might have put my ship on that ledge. Pass Bird Rock to starboard; give it a wide berth.

Beyond Bird Rock, I set a course of 010° true on The Twins, two islets a couple of miles west of the mouth of Hobart Bay. This carried me well away from the horrible mid-channel mishmash of rocks and islets called The Five Fingers. When I was about a half-mile from The Twins, I got out Chart 17363, turned to starboard, approached the southern side of Entrance Island, discovered the doorway to the dogleg cove, very slowly slid into it, turned to port and—*voila!*—found what must be the snuggest state-operated float in all of Southeast Alaska. I had come 45 miles from Petersburg.

I wrote something a couple of paragraphs back about 'floating' obstacles in Stephens Passage. I didn't mean logs. I meant icebergs. I doubt very much if you will run into them (I should hope you *never* would run into them) on the route just described from Petersburg to Entrance Island. You are quite likely to see them and come very close to them, however, on the run north from Entrance Island. I'll write more about those icebergs in the next chapter.

There are a couple of alternate anchorages that should be mentioned:

—Cleveland Passage, the water way between Whitney Island and the mainland. It offers good anchorage near its southeast end. After swinging around Bird Rock, set a course to clear Whitney's Bill Point, then turn sharply to starboard and take a mid-channel direction into Cleveland Passage. Run for about two miles until your depthfinder indicates about eight fathoms. Anchor here for fairly good protection from strong winds. Beware of the nasty rock at the southern end of the passage.

—Cannery Cove, Pybus Bay, on the western side of Stephens

Passage. I never have been there, but the Coast Pilot indicates it is a snug anchorage in six fathoms over a sticky bottom. I certainly wouldn't attempt maneuvering among all those baring rocks and islets without Chart 17363.

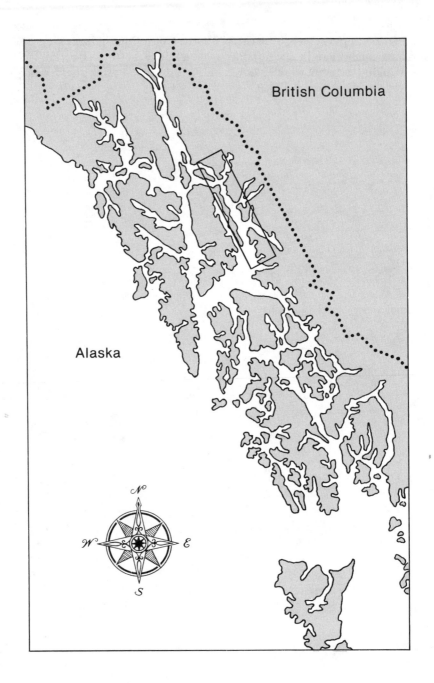

British Columbia

Alaska

Entrance
Island
To Juneau

You should have U.S. Charts 17360 (Etolin Island to Midway Islands; 1:217,828 scale), 17300 (Stephens Passage to Cross Sound; 1:209,978 scale), and 17315 (Gastineau Channel and Taku Inlet; 1:40,000 scale).

It indeed will be a most unusual summer in Southeast Alaska if, on this run, you do not see plenty of the floating icebergs mentioned in the last chapter. In my initial trip to the Panhandle in 1982, I first saw them in Stephens Passage when my ship was northbound in the general vicinity of Hobart Bay. What attracted my attention was a large, white object about a dozen miles away off the southern end of the Glass Peninsula, on the western side of the passage. Must be quite a good-sized cruiser, I mused, but it doesn't seem to be moving. A few minutes later, I realized I was looking at a number of those good-sized, white cruisers. That's when I got out the binoculars and identified my first iceberg.

The icebergs come from the Dawes Glacier, at the head of Endicott Arm, 30 miles from the mouth of Holkam Bay, and/or from the Sawyer Glaciers, 25 miles from Holkham Bay at the head of Tracy Arm. Currents carry the 'growlers' —some huge, some small—to the bay which, according to the Coast Pilot, always contains some of them. Many are grounded on shoals in the bay. Tidal currents carry the still floating ones out into Stephens Passage where they drift for many miles, both north and south of the bay. In the summer of 1982, I saw them all the way from south of the Glass Peninsula to a point well north of the Midway Islands, a distance of at least 25 miles.

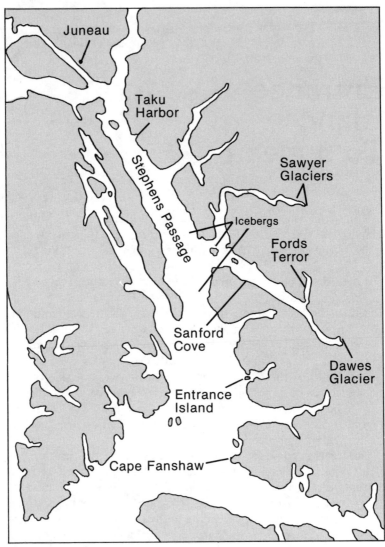

Iceberg Country

The closer you come to them, the more you realize that those beautiful postcard-colored pictures of blue-white icebergs were not fakes. Don't get too close, at least with your ship. You are looking at only the top one-tenth of an iceberg, and you really don't know how extensive the rest of the shape is, or where it is. A dinghy should be used if you are going to collect some cocktail ice. As far as navigation among icebergs is concerned, cruise in Stephens Passage only in clear daylight. The icebergs are a dangerous, serious menace to navigation at night or in fog.

Long, straight runs will get you to Juneau. Just be sure to dodge all those icebergs. Swing away from Entrance Island, keeping The Twins and Sunset Island to port, then steer off Point League and fix a course to pass the Midway Islands to port. Head for Grave Point; it is easily identified by Taku Mountain, a 2,139-foot eminence that rises abruptly just north of the point. Don't trust your compass in the vicinity of Grave Point because of a local magnetic disturbance. Skirt Grave Point and set a course that will keep Grave Island and Point Arden to port. Enter Gastineau Channel.

Gastineau is free of mid-channel hazards for the first half-dozen miles. When you have the Douglas small-boat basin abeam to port, slow down and take care ahead. Filling more than one-half of Gastineau Channel from its northeast side is an enormous rock dump, the tailings of a once-flourishing gold mine. The red buoy guarding it must be kept to starboard; the navigable channel in this vicinity is reduced to about 400 yards; keep a sharp watch for large cruise ships and state ferries.

Call the Juneau harbormaster on the VHF; his office monitors Channel 16 from 0800 to 1630 daily. He controls berthage at three harbors with space for more than 900 small craft. You might think this would be enough, but it isn't, particularly in the summer if the fishing fleets are not working. In two visits to Juneau, I was accommodated once and told to fend for myself the other time. The places he controls are these: Harris Harbor, just barely north of the Juneau-Douglas bridge with the entrance requiring a sharp turn to starboard immediately after clearing the bridge; the newer, larger Aurora Basin, 0.3 mile north of the bridge with entrances at either end of a long, detached breakwater, and the Douglas basin, a couple of miles south of the bridge on the Douglas Island, or southwest side, of Gastineau Channel.

At any event, hot damn! You have made it all the way from Seattle to Alaska's capital! You have done something few other pleasureboaters accomplish. If you stuck to the suggested daily cruising plans in this book, it has taken you 20 days. You came 65 miles today from Entrance Island and that, by golly, was the longest run of them all (by one mile; Oliver Cove to Butedale was 64 miles). The average daily run was 47.6 miles. And you have come a grand total of 952 miles, which just goes to show that Woodward certainly can lead you astray; the shortest official 'inside' route from Seattle to Juneau is 879 miles.

There are several exciting dawdling places and alternate anchorages between Entrance Island and Juneau. Here is a run down on some of them:

—Taku Harbor, 20 miles south of Juneau at Grave Point. It is a famed place if there ever was one in Southeast Alaska. Both Father Hubbard, the 'glacier priest' and Tiger Olson, a legendary hermit, lived there. A state-operated float is located off the eastern shore 0.8 mile inside the harbor's entrance. Some skippers prefer to turn more sharply to starboard after rounding Stockade Point for an anchorage in two or three fathoms; they may obtain better protection from some winds in that location. A crab pot, placed off the western shore, close to the estuary, might produce. Halibut can be caught in the harbor. Salmon fishing sometimes is excellent along the kelp beds north of Grave Point.

—Sanford Cove, Holkham Bay. Enter Holkham Bay by passing north of the Wood Spit light, shown on a tower with a red triangular daymark; there is about a half-mile of deep water between the light and the southern end of the reef extending southeast from Harbor Island. A southeasterly course into Endicott Arm from the light for 4.5 miles will bring you to Sanford Cove. By careful use of the depthfinder, you can locate an anchorage in about seven fathoms close to shore. Be wary of icebergs both in entering Holkham Bay and after anchoring in Sanford Cove. Tidal currents may run as strong as four knots in the bay and swirls are reported, making the presence of icebergs more than just interesting. Sanford Cove is used by some skippers as a base for explorations into both Endicott Arm and Tracy Arm. The Sumdum

132

Glacier, receding and no longer depositing icebergs into salt water, is a magnificent sight to the east at the entrance to Holkham Bay.

—Fords Terror, a short fjord off the eastern side of Endicott Arm about 16 miles from Holkham Bay. This phenomenon is extremely well-named, but its reward is a dramatic trip through a marine canyon; the Coast Pilot, not known for its lyrical prose, praises the 'magnificent scenery' of Fords Terror. But it also warns of a highly dangerous hazard, a narrows located less than two miles inside the entrance to the fjord. The low-water depth is less than two feet; that is correct, less than two feet! And currents rush with great velocity through it. The only time—repeat: the only time—to transit the narrows is at high water slack. This means an overnight anchorage in Fords Terror. The depths are large and the only chart available—17360—is of no help. Skippers simply are reduced to nosing around close to shore with the depthfinders working to find resting places. And most of them discover that their VHF radio reception is zilch in Fords Terror. One consolation, in addition to the scenery: no icebergs.

—Dawes Glacier, 30 miles from Holkham Bay at the end of Endicott Arm. This is a calving glacier, and its spawn may prevent you from reaching the face of the glacier. There is no anchorage.

—The Sawyer Glaciers, 25 miles from Holkham Bay at the two ends of Tracy Arm. The navigable entrance to Tracy Arm is about 400 yards wide with rocky shoals on both sides. Neither of the shoals is marked by an aid to navigation, but there is a range on the northwest end of Harbor Island that is in line with a daybeacon on the east shore of Tracy Arm. If the arm is not clogged with icebergs, it is possible to run the entire length of this twisting, highly scenic fjord. South Sawyer Glacier usually is the most active. The Coast Pilot reports that huge chunks of ice breaking from the glacier have caused waves as high as 25 feet. There is no anchorage.

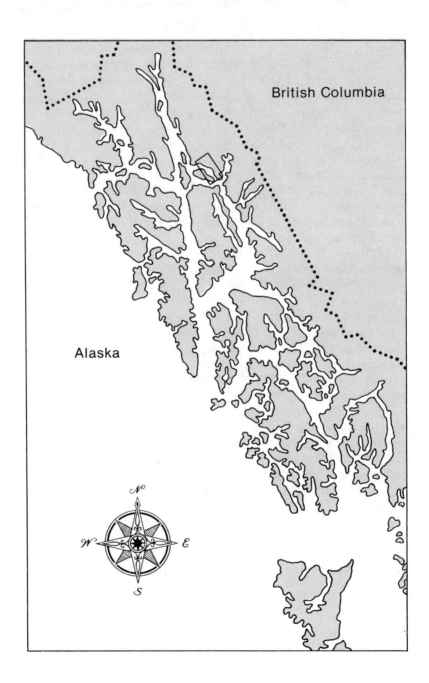

British Columbia

Alaska

Quo Vadis?

Unless I greatly misunderstand your situation, the answer to where you now will go from Juneau hangs mostly on the amount of time you have left for dawdling. Most pleasureboaters simply don't have three or four weeks to dedicate. It would be my guess that the average skipper, having arrived at Juneau, finds that he really has only about a couple of weeks in which to nose around in the Panhandle before he must head for home. Another factor is the available good weather; I do not think that it would be wise to tarry in Southeast Alaska so long that September will impinge on the return trip; the likelihood of fog in Queen Charlotte Sound, for example, gets progressively worse after July; August is 'iffy'; September is not good.

The rest of this book will be devoted to helping you accomplish the excursions possible within your time constraints. It certainly will not be a complete guide. Far from it. It would take another entire book to detail all the exciting, enticing and beautiful spots to which a pleasureboater could go in the vast Panhandle. But there are some places that appear, with very good reason, to be more popular than others. Those places would include some we already have discussed—Wrangell, Petersburg and environs, Holkham Bay and its icebergs, and Taku Harbor.

They certainly also would include Skagway, Glacier Bay, Sitka, various hot springs and other inlet enticements off Chatham Strait, and the Behm Canal, near Ketchikan. Depending on the speed of the boat and the dawdling desires of its cap'n and crew, all the attractions in this latter group could be visited, briefly, in from two to three weeks. By that, I mean they could be seen in a tense, tiring two weeks, and at a slightly more leisurely pace in three. Even at three weeks, there wouldn't be much time for lazily picking the lint from one's belly button, if you know what I mean.

Let's start with the least available amount of time. If all you have is less than a week, I think you'd do well just to turn around and head south, taking in some of the alternative anchorages you missed coming north, doing some fishing, then spending two or three days swinging clockwise in the Behm Canal; at the conclusion of the Behm Canal circuit you would be in a position to recross Dixon Entrance.

All the others—Skagway, Glacier Bay, Sitka and the inlets of Chatham Strait—can be accomplished consecutively by going north, west and then south from Juneau. Such a consecutive swing would leave you within a day's run of Petersburg and the start of your long southerly trek. Some of the segments can be omitted; for example, you are not required to go either to Skagway or to Glacier Bay in order to get to Sitka, and you don't need to visit Sitka in order to poke into the inlets of Chatham Strait. The entire, consecutive swing would be a grand odyssey, one you'd never forget. But maybe you can do only part of it. To help you decide which portions you will try, here is a very brief rundown on the approximate required time plus a sketchy picture of what you would enjoy in each segment:

—Skagway, at the head of Lynn Canal. Skagway is 100 miles from Juneau; an 80-mile return run would put you in Funter Bay, ready to move out to Glacier Bay or on to Sitka or Chatham Strait. If the winds are calm (a big factor), I suppose you could race up to Skagway and back in three days; four days would be much better. Attractions: a multitude of glaciers and waterfalls seen from an ever-narrowing Lynn Canal, a huge bald eagle nesting area near Haines, and the gold rush days atmosphere of Skagway. (Be advised, however, that the cliff-hanging, narrow-gauge railway that links Skagway with Whitehorse at the other end of the Klondike Trail ceased passenger service in 1982; a bus trip was substituted.)

—Glacier Bay, out to the west through Icy Strait. From Juneau, Funter Bay is 50 miles, Bartlett Cove in Glacier Bay another 45. You'd need a day, at least, to get up into and enjoy the bay's fantastic glacier areas; two would be much better.

136

On the return, it is 60 miles or so from the mouth of Glacier Bay to Tenakee Springs, one of Chatham Strait's inlet attractions and a way stop on the route to Sitka. What would you need to 'do' Glacier Bay? Anywhere from three to six days, I should think.

—Sitka, via Peril Strait and Sergius Narrows. From Juneau, Funter Bay is 50 miles, Tenakee Springs another 35, and Sitka another 80 or so. Tenakee Springs is a noted spa (noted in a different sort of way; definite hours for females and males, and never the twain shall meet). The 'inside' route to Sitka is a challenging and beautiful thing through wooded, narrow, current-swirling channels; the goal is Southeast Alaska's most beautiful city, one laden with historical native and Russian impacts. It might require two days on the return trip to get from Sitka to Warm Springs Bay, another kind of spa on the eastern side of Baranof Island. All told, I guess, the Sitka jaunt would require from five to seven days.

—Interesting inlets on Chatham Strait. I've already mentioned Funter Bay, a (once?) famed crabbing area, Tenakee Springs, and Warm Springs Bay. Farther south there is Red Bluff Bay, a marine canyon you won't believe unless you poke your ship into it. All along the way, awe-inspiring waterfalls and mountain vistas will inspire you, to say nothing of cavorting humpback whales. To just 'do' Chatham Strait from Juneau would take a day each to Funter, Tenakee, Warm Springs and Red Bluff Bays—a total of four days without any tarrying. At Red Bluff Bay, you'd only be 55 miles from Portage Bay, near Petersburg, and the start of your run to Behm Canal and/or home.

—Behm Canal, a 100-mile, almost hazard-free waterway skirting the west, north and east sides of Revillagigedo Island. Island-dotted bays; a warm springs resort; narrow inlets with precipitous sides; a startling, 230-foot high midchannel rock, plus good fishing, would make a clockwise tour of Behm Canal a fitting finale for your visit to Southeast Alaska. Two days; three would be better.

From all the above, I hope you can determine what you will be able to do in the time left for you in the Panhandle. Subsequent chapters will attempt to meet the navigation challenges on each of the above segments.

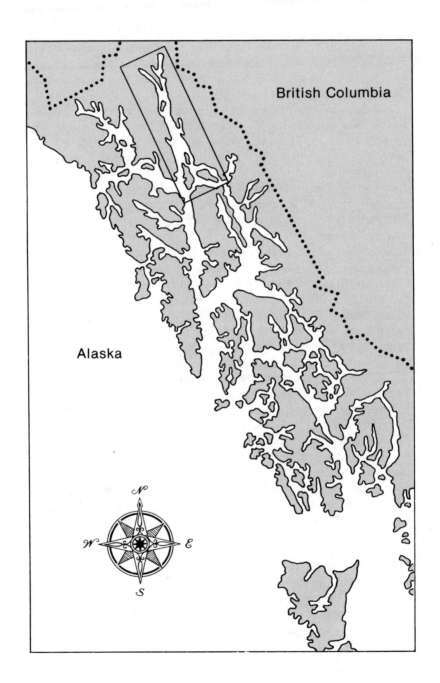

British Columbia

Alaska

Skagway
(And Funter Bay)

You should have U.S. Charts 17315 (Gastineau Channel and Taku Inlet; 1:40,000 scale), 17316 (Lynn Canal, from Icy Strait to Point Sherman; 1:80,000 scale) and 17317 (Lynn Canal—Point Sherman to Skagway; 1:80,000 scale).

There are two factors with potential to make a run to Skagway difficult. One is wind, and the only solution is to make sure you monitor closely the weather forecasts both before leaving Juneau and while en route, having in mind at all times where the nearest hole-in-the-wall is. The other is distance; 100 miles is too long and tiring for a one-day run for most of us; that problem can be solved, however, by noting that Echo Bay, a tight extension of Berners Bay, is almost exactly at the halfway mark of that 100-mile trip.

As to wind, we might as well begin with the worst possible scenario under the theory that things can't help but get better. The truth is that, in the winter, northerly blasts often attain speeds of 70 knots in wind-funneling Lynn Canal. While that extreme violence is not likely to occur in good weather months, it still is true that strong summer winds—some mariners call them 'williwaws'—can and do come whistling through the canal with wave-rolling effect. If there ever was a prolonged wind funnel, Lynn Canal is it. Six miles wide at its southern end, it is patrolled by 6,000-foot mountains closely on both sides as it gradually narrows to one mile near Skagway. That can mean only one thing: whatever wind is blowing will be intensified in the canal. So keep your ear tuned to that continuous weather broadcast and know where the nearest harbor of refuge is.

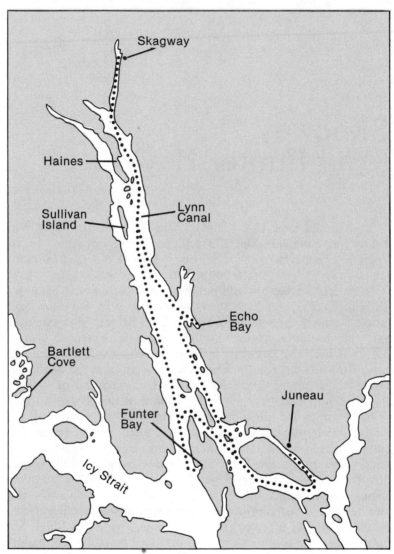

To Skagway
And/Or Funter Bay

To go north to Skagway from Juneau, turn south. I wash my hands of your whole cruise if you plan to escape by going north over the frightfully shallow Mendenhall Bar. True, it is 18 miles shorter that way and it can be done with local knowledge at high water; what's more, seasonal buoys are placed in an effort to mark the shifting channels. I'll have no part of it. I say the way to leave Juneau for the north is to go south until you can skirt Marmion Island and Point Tantallon to enter Stephens Passage. Strike off for Point Hilda, then follow the Douglas Island shore to avoid Dernin Rock north of Outer Point.

(Note to those not aiming for Skagway and only seeking Funter Bay: when off Outer Point on Douglas Island, swerve to port to enter Saginaw Channel. Keep Favorite Reef to starboard and make sure you have cleared all of the Barlow Islands before swinging more to port to pass between Point Retreat and Faust Rock. You probably will be in a covey of intent sportsfishermen; this is a hot salmon area. Work your way around Point Retreat and begin your southbound course to Funter Bay. Beware of the North Ledge, Naked Island and The Kittens when approaching the entrance to Funter Bay. Most mariners will seek the free-floating, state-operated float off the eastern shore about a mile from the bay's entrance. In good weather, the float is all right, but winds can sweep into the bay from both the south and west. In that event, a calmer place would be to anchor deep in Crab Cove. Sure, put down your crab pots. Lots of luck. It once was a famed place for crabs, but I fear the resource is depleted badly due to intense pressure from both commercial and sports interests.)

The Skagway-bound skipper will move from Outer Point through Favorite Channel by keeping Portland Island close to port with Aaron, Bird and Gull Islands to starboard. Take a midchannel heading between Sentinel and Benjamin Island, and put North Island to starboard as you enter Lynn Canal. Steer for a point about one-half mile off Point Bridget, the southern guardian of the entrance to Berners Bay. Maintain that one-half-mile distance off shore as you turn east at the point and run for about one mile. Slow down and crawl into Echo Bay, using your depthfinder and Chart 17316 to locate that close-to-shore, very narrow channel at the bay's mouth. Go deep into the bay for a four-fathom, secure anchorage.

There is little I can add to what the chart plainly shows for the route between Echo Bay and Skagway. The chart advertises well the relatively few hazards. Probably your compass will be wildly off in Chilkoot Inlet due to a local magnetic disturbance. Both Haines and Skagway have small craft basins in the charge of harbormasters.

Funter Bay is about 78 miles from Skagway. If this is too much for a one-day run, acceptable anchorage can be found in the bight west of the south end of Sullivan Island. This bight is 45 miles from Funter Bay. At any event, off Point Sherman on the southbound run from Skagway, set a course that will carry you about a mile off Point Whitney. This should bring you in Lynn Canal to the mouth of Funter Bay.

Skagway (and Funter Bay)

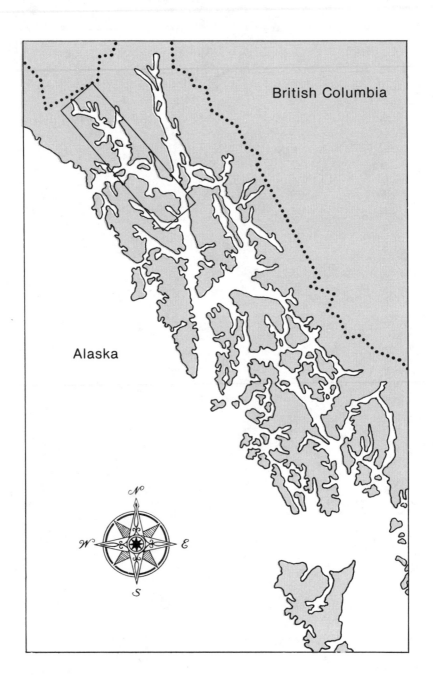

British Columbia

Alaska

Glacier Bay
(And Tenakee Springs)

You should have U.S. Charts 17300 (Stephens Passage to Cross Sound; 1:209,978 scale); 17316 (Lynn Canal, from Icy Strait to Point Sherman); 17302 (Icy Strait and Cross Sound), and 17318 (Glacier Bay); the latter three all are 1:80,000 scale.

And you *must* have permission from Uncle Sam to enter Glacier Bay. He isn't afraid you'll walk off with one of his 16 active tidewater glaciers that make the bay such a spectacular place. But he is worried about humpback whales. They once cavorted in great numbers in Glacier Bay, but now are down to a dozen or so animals. Uncle believes that too many pleasure boats nudging around in the humpbacks' feeding grounds may be an adverse factor.

So the whole thing now is Glacier Bay National Park (including the water), and the National Park Service admits no more than 21 pleasure boats to the bay at any one time. In 1984, this limitation period ran from June 1 through August 31. Application for a permit may be made by mail to Superintendent, Glacier Bay National Park, Gustavus, Alaska 99826; by telephone to (907) 697-3522, or by VHF radio on Channel 16 to KWM-20, Bartlett Cove, between 0800 and 1600 daily. Do not write more than 60 days or less than 30 days prior to your proposed entry date. For less than 30 days prior to entry, telephone or use the VHF radio. Information required for a permit: boat name and number, skipper's name, address, and telephone number; brief description of vessel, proposed date of entry with first, second and third choices, number of persons aboard, number of days desired (the maximum is seven days). Permits must

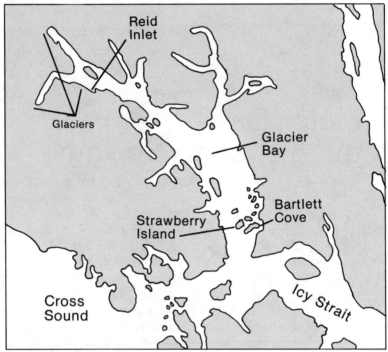

Among The Glaciers

be confirmed within 48 hours of entry; permits not confirmed by 1000 on entry date will be cancelled.

Yes, big cruise ships and commercial fishing vessels also enter Glacier Bay. They are regulated by a different set of rules.

After obtaining a permit, your next concern should be Icy Strait, through which you must pass to reach Glacier Bay. The Strait, and something called Cross Sound, actually compose one bow-shaped, east-west, 60-mile-long waterway that is the northernmost connection from the Pacific Ocean to the Panhandle's inland channels. The Inian Islands, about ten miles from the Pacific, do a fairly good job of breaking the ocean's swells and serve as the dividing line for the nomenclature; Cross Sound lies to the west of the islands, Icy Strait to the east. Lemesurier Island, a large mass in midchannel just west of the entrance to Glacier Bay, also helps to dampen ocean swells. Still, particularly after a fierce storm in the Gulf of Alaska, swells can be felt in Icy Strait east of Glacier Bay. It also is possible, but not too likely in the summer, that you may find icebergs in Icy Strait. What you definitely can expect, however, are strong currents and tide rips off the entrance to Glacier Bay. Strong currents (at times reaching six knots) probably will continue into the bay as far as Willoughby Island, some dozen miles north of the bay's entrance. Vigorous currents also can be expected in Bartlett Cove, five miles from the entrance and probably the site of your first night's anchorage in the bay.

In view of all the above, it is obvious that weather will be a prime factor. Monitor the forecasts and don't go if winds above 15 knots are predicted for Icy Strait.

To reach Glacier Bay from Funter Bay, move southwesterly across Lynn Canal and pass between Point Couverden and Rocky Island. Set a course to keep the Pleasant Island Reef buoy to starboard and enter Glacier Bay in mid-channel. In 1984, this midchannel entry, rather than a more normal course close to the eastern shore, was required by the National Park Service as a whale protection regulation. In fact, mid-channel courses also were required in gaining Bartlett Cove and in Glacier Bay, itself, as far as the north end of Strawberry Island. Steady speed less than ten knots in those same areas also was a 1984 rule.

Bartlett Cove itself is not the greatest anchorage in the world being open to southwest winds, but good holding ground in seven fathoms can be found about 400 yards off its southeast side near the National Park Service pier. To the southwest of this pier, there are floats controlled by a lodge operated by a concessionaire; unless you plan to be a patron-paying customer of the lodge, you will not be welcome at the concessionaire's floats. You will be more than welcome, however, at the Park Service headquarters, close to the federal pier. Rangers there are anxious to be of service; their advice as to where to go from Bartlett Cove will be up-to-date and practical.

Navigation in Glacier Bay is a challenging thing. Icebergs abound. Swirls and eddies, some of them caused by unpredictable freshwater intrusions from the glaciers, are common. Fog can be expected, particularly in late summer. Both authorities—the Park Service and the Coast Pilot—warn that the faces of glaciers should not be approached closer than one-half mile to be safe from huge waves generated by gigantic chunks of ice breaking from the glaciers. To top it all, there is this grim warning in the Coast Pilot: "Vessels are advised to carry extra propellers aboard when navigating Glacier Bay and single-screw vessels should not attempt to navigate the bay at all." How about that!?

Still, it is done; prudent skippers can and do enjoy moving into the far reaches of Glacier Bay. Perhaps one of the better anchorages for basing an exploration of a good portion of the bay is to be found in Reid Inlet, about 45 miles into the bay from Bartlett Cove. The safest route is to move in mid-channel past Strawberry Island, then keep Drake Island and tiny Lone Island to port. Continue a mid-channel course around Gilbert Peninsula, then begin to close in on the southern shoreline. The entrance to Reid Inlet, a half-mile southwest of Ibach Point, is partially blocked by gravel bars extending from both shores to form a 200-yard-wide entrance channel with three fathoms at low water. If you can, enter at low water. Find a snug anchorage south of the dollop of an island close to the west side of the inlet. There is floating ice in the inlet, but little of it reaches the west side. Have fun ashore by examining the abandoned wooden dwellings of a once flourishing mining operation. In Reid Inlet, you are less than two miles from Reid Glacier and a scant 15 miles from the Grand Pacific Glacier at the head of Tarr Inlet. The mouth of the mighty Johns Hopkins Glacier is

148

about ten miles away, but its inlet is likely to be chuckablock with floating ice.

When it comes time to leave Glacier Bay, do not forget the requirement to check out with the National Park Service. This can be done in person at Bartlett Cove or by VHF as you leave. In retracing your steps in Icy Strait, don't get over to the Chichagof Island shore until you have cleared Spasski Island and its ugly rock pile. Swing rather closely around Point Augusta, North Passage Point and East Point to gain Tenakee Inlet. Follow the north shore of the inlet for about nine miles, paying close heed to the aids to navigation, and then slowly work your way over to the state-operated floats that are a half-mile or so east of the prominent city pier at which there is no float moorage. If the floats are crowded, indifferent moorage can be had alongside the floating breakwater, but you'll have to use your dinghy to get ashore. A trail—'Tenakee Avenue', if you please—will take you into beautiful, downtown Tenakee Springs and its public, free (donations accepted gladly), sex-segregated, warm springs facility. Don't be too fooled by the 'traffic light' at the intersection of Tenakee Avenue and the city pier, but it is typical of this fiercely independent, but good-humored community.

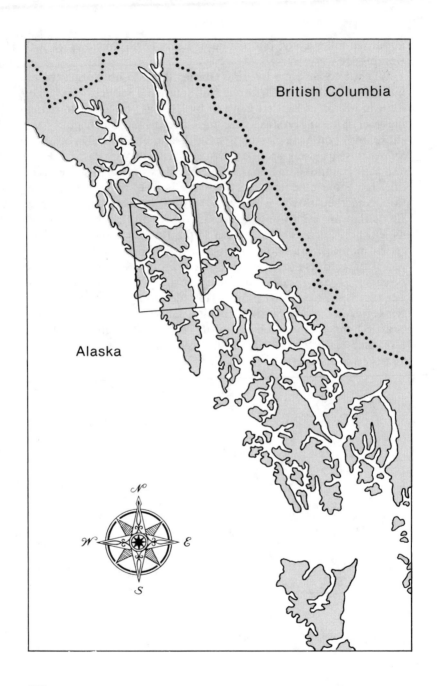

British Columbia

Alaska

Sitka

You should have U.S. Charts 17320 (Coronation Island to Lisianski Strait; 1:217,828 scale); 17338 (Peril Strait; 1:40,000 scale); 17323 (Salisbury Sound and Peril Strait, 1:40,000 scale); 17324 (Sitka Sound to Salisbury Sound; 1:40,000 scale), and 17327 (Sitka Harbor; 1:10,000 scale), and you must be able to determine the time of slack water in Sergius Narrows, and the direction and strength of the current in Peril, Neva and Olga Straits.

There are a couple of reasons why the run from Tenakee Springs to Sitka should be a two-day affair. One is that the distance is 80 miles. The other is that you are almost sure to need a layover cove in which to await the correct time to slip through Sergius Narrows.

I am partial to Nismeni Cove, having twice enjoyed its protection from southerly winds. A 53-mile run from Tenakee Springs, it is ideally placed in Peril Strait, being notched into the Duffield Peninula of Baranof Island exactly where the strait begins its narrow, current-ridden southwesterly course. In addition, Nismeni is easy to enter. There are other layover places and I'll talk about them, but Nismeni may be the best of the bunch.

From Tenakee Springs, run out of the inlet along its northern side. The safer turn at South Passage Point would be to keep the Tenakee Inlet Entrance light to starboard. Stay about one mile off the Chichagof Island shore as you move south for 20 miles, watching for offshore hazards south of White Rock. By all means, keep clear of Morris Reef, a bottom-busting place of ledges and submerged rocks. Keep the reef's lighted buoy to starboard as you swing around it to enter Peril Strait.

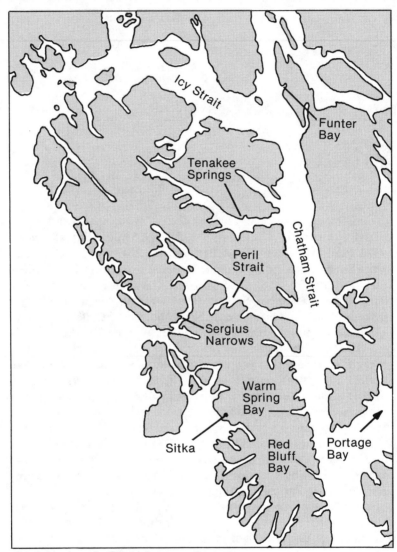

Sitka And Chatham Strait

In this neighborhood—the intersection of Peril and Chatham Straits—watch closely for humpback whales. You will experience a real thrill when you see the entire lunging hulk of a 40-foot humpback come out of the water, then crash back into it with an enormous splash. If you do see such a sight, what you witness probably is the animal's effort to rid itself of barnacles.

Run along the northern shore of Peril Strait until you are past False Lindenberg Head, then diagonally cross the strait with a course that will keep you about a half-mile off Pescham Point. Staying in deep water, work around the Duffield Peninsula shore and enter Nismeni Cove by favoring its southern side. Anchor in the middle of the cove in about seven fathoms.

There are three other acceptable anchorages to the east of Nismeni Cove. Saook Bay I used once; someone told me about running deep, but I did not like the looks of all those shallow flats, so we anchored near the mouth of the bay in about five fathoms close to the northern shore; Nismeni was better, I thought. Then there is Rodman Bay, but why run six miles to its anchorable head? On the south side of Rodman Bay, however, is Appleton Cove; if you carefully pick your way past Prince Island with your depthfinder going full blast, you can find a snug anchorage; more difficult to enter than Nismeni, but perhaps better after you get there.

There is one more—Deep Bay, on the west side of the narrow portion of Peril Strait some 11 miles south of Nismeni Cove. It is a dandy anchorage and is only two miles from Sergius Narrows. But you'd have to diddle with the current tables twice, once to get to Deep Bay, and once on the next day to get through Sergius. At Nismeni, you'll only need one session with the current tables.

And you must have that session. Make no mistake about it, Sergius Narrows should be navigated for the first time by an inexperienced skipper only a high water slack; positively and without any exception, only a high water slack! It can be a piece of cake then and you undoubtedly will wonder what all the fussing was about. Let's see if I can quickly command your respect of Sergius. In the first place, it is one of only four passes listed in the Pacific Coast Tidal Current Tables for special statistical treatment; the others are Deception Pass, Seymour Narrows and Isanotski Strait. All of them are awesome in the sudden and sustained way that maximum currents surge through them. The critical portion of Sergius is just 450 feet long, the length of the dredged channel that is 24 feet deep and only 300 feet wide. One side of the channel is the rock wall of Sergius Point; the other, marked by nun buoys, includes a covered rock and a submerged ledge. Through this aperture race mighty and variable-direction currents of almost six knots on the flood and 5.5 knots at the ebb.

At slack water, however, the thing is a mill pond for about ten minutes, plenty of time to get through. The only problem then would be other ships waiting for the same slack period. An Alaska state ferry can fill most of the channel. The thing to do is to arrive in your southbound ship at Bear Bay, slightly more than a mile north of the narrows, a half-hour prior to your computed time of high water slack. From Bear Bay you not only can see any competing traffic, but you also can ascertain the positions of the buoys in the narrows. Their attitudes are critical; if they are perpendicular, go. If any of them is horizontal, or nearly so, wait. On a northbound run, the same sort of waiting game can be played by halting your ship just north of Suloia Point about 30 minutes ahead of the slack water prediction time.

At Nismeni Cove, Sergius Narrows is not quite 13 miles away. You will need to consult the Current Tables to learn how the current will affect the over-the-bottom speed of your ship so that you will accomplish your scheduled arrival time at Bear Bay. The average maximum velocity of the current between Sergius Narrows and the northern end of the narrow portion of Peril Strait is around two knots. Chart 17323 gives a clear picture of the hazards and aids to navigation in that run, plus a 1:20,000-scale blow-up of the narrows. I can't add anything helpful to those excellent charts except this obvious warning: beware of those nasty rocks off Nismeni Point when leaving the cove.

After negotiating Sergius Narrows, slip through Kakul Narrows and around the buoy off Point Kakul. For the time it will take your ship to negotiate the three miles from Point Kakul to the Kane Islands at the northern end of Neva Strait, you may experience ocean swells, for you will be crossing Salisbury Sound; the open ocean is only a half-dozen miles to the west. The 1:20,000-scale enlargement of Neva Strait on Chart 17324 should get you through without difficulty; note the range, 'backward' on the southbound run, to be used in negotiating Whitestone Narrows. Current should not be a problem in either Neva or Olga Straits; the maximum velocities rarely exceed 1.5 knots.

After clearing Olga Strait, swing fairly close along the Lisianski Peninsula shore until you have the north end of Big Gravanski Island abeam to starboard. Come right enough to pass the Old Sitka Rocks light well to port, then dive between the Kasiana Islands and the Baranof Island shore and make a mid-channel approach between the channel buoys just south of Watson Point. Get out Chart 17327 for a detailed guide into Sitka's harbor.

Along about this point, or earlier, you might try calling the Sitka harbormaster on the VHF. Lots of luck. The one thing that may mar what should be your otherwise pleasant visit to historic and beautiful Sitka is the great lack of transient float space. You will be lucky, indeed, if you are not required to raft out—perhaps several boats away from the float—in the meager small-boat basin just north of the graceful bridge to Japonski Island. Look with envy, if you will, at the fabulous city-owned Crescent Bay marina around to the east and south of the bridge; there may be vacancies, but the harbormaster, with a stern hand, enforces a strict 'no-transient' rule there. It's for the home folks. Period.

On the return trip, it is more than 80 miles from Sitka via Peril Strait to Warm Spring Bay. The journey can become a two-day thing with an anchorage at any of the resting places already discussed in this chapter. For a spot on the southern side of Sergius Narrows, Schulze Cove, 1½-miles east of Suloia Point, provides a secure anchorage; it is used as a log storage area, but usually there is room to skirt the booms and get into an anchoring area. It was at Schulze Cove one misty morning that I got my one and only look at two wild Alaska brown bears, ponderously patrolling the beach not too far from my anchored ship.

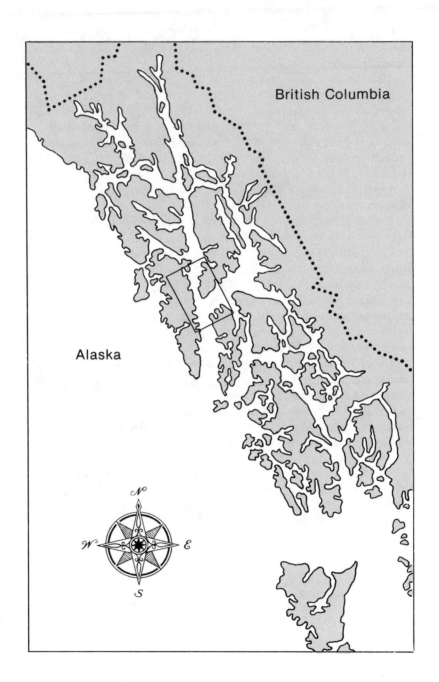

British Columbia

Alaska

Two Bays
In Chatham
Strait,
And On Toward
The Behm Canal

You should have U.S. Charts 17320 (Coronation Island to Lisianski Strait; 1:217,828 scale), 17337 (Harbors in Chatham Strait and Vicinity, including Warm Spring Bay, 1:20,000 scale); 17336 (Harbors in Chatham Strait and Vicinity, including Red Bluff Bay, 1:20,000 scale); 17360 (Etolin Island to Midway Islands; 1:217,828 scale), and 17367 (Thomas, Farragut and Portage Bays, 1:40,000 scale).

Warm Spring Bay (a thundering waterfall close to your moorage, a hot tub soak, and excellent fishing) and Red Bluff Bay (a marine canyon you won't believe until you see it plus, perhaps, a mess of shrimp in your crab trap) are two indentations of the east coast of Baranof Island that you should not miss. They are easily reached on your way south from Skagway, Glacier Bay and/or Sitka.

Distances to Warm Spring Bay are these: from Tenakee Springs, 43 miles; from Schulze Cove, just south of Sergius Narrows, 50 miles; from Nismeni Cove, 37 miles. On the run south in Chatham Strait, there is very little to do except keep about a half-mile off the Baranof Island shore and enjoy the spectacular scenery of towering, snow-covered mountain peaks and plunging waterfalls. Just south of Takatz Bay set a course directly on the light guarding the southern entrance to Warm Spring Bay. Hold that course until you have a clear sight into the inner bay, turn to starboard and head for the spectacular waterfall less than two miles away.

There is a float and pier at the tiny community of Baranof. Either side can be used, but entrance to the inner or shore side is

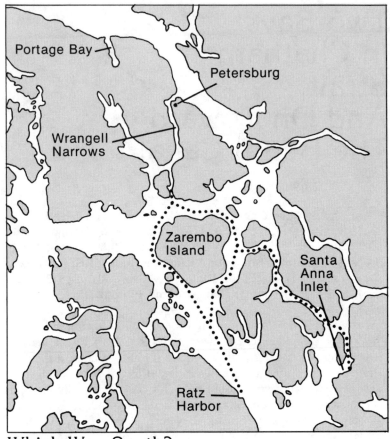

Which Way South?

tricky; avoid the rock east of the float's end. If you lie to the outer side, the current from the waterfall, only 200 yards away, will tend to hold you to the float; the contrary, of course, will be true on the inner side of the float. If the float is too crowded (mini-cruise ships frequent the place and often take up much space), either of the two coves on the south side of the bay can be used for anchoring; the more easterly one is open to northerly winds.

Climb the gangway to the pier and at the general store rent, for a modest fee, one of the long, deep tubs in private stalls for a relaxing, hot, mineral water soak. Trout are caught off the waterfall and in the salt water lagoon. Sea bass, red snapper, salmon and halibut are likely catches off the mouth of the bay.

When you can tear yourself away from Warm Spring Bay, run for 15 miles south along the Baranof Island shore to Red Bluff Bay. You can't miss it; it is guarded on its northern side by a 550-foot brick red eminence, the only one like it in the vicinity. The entrance is somewhat exciting, but easy. Run south beyond the mess of islands apparently clogging the bay's entrance. Turn to starboard and sneak along the steep, heavily wooded southern shoreline of the bay until you have cleared all the islands. Then run for 2½ miles deep into the bay with its towering sheer walls on both sides. Find the little peninsula on the northern side east of the estuary; anchor in the bight formed by the peninsula in about four fathoms. Before the sun goes down (it will do that suddenly and dramatically), row over to the south side of the estuary and dunk whatever traps you have. I confidently put down a crab trap there in 20 feet of water. The next morning I pulled the trap, but was not too disappointed to find no crabs because it held 75 big shrimp! I guess that sort of knocks in the head the idea that you must get into deep water to snag shrimp. I hope you do as well.

Yes, there are other dramatic bays indenting Chatham Strait. But before you plunge on southward, note three things: (1) Chatham Strait, which is only five miles wide off Warm Spring Bay, has a girth three times that at its southern end; (2) the strait's southern end merges with the wide open Pacific Ocean, and (3) if you do make it, say, to Port Alexander, an interesting fishing community almost at the southern tip of Baranof Island, you either must retrace your southbound steps or face a 25-mile crossing of the strait to get around Cape Decision to enter Sumner Strait. I did that once. I never need to do it again. It was far worse than anything either Dixon Entrance of Queen Charlotte Sound ever did to me and my ship.

At Red Bluff Bay I am assuming that you are ready to head for the barn with, perhaps, a swing around the Behm Canal before leaving Alaska. It's easy. Set a northeasterly course and drive across Chatham Strait to enter your old friend, Frederick Sound. Watch for the longline buoys of commercial halibut fishermen. Head for Turnabout Island and when about two miles away pass between it and the Pinta Rocks. Then simply stay about a half-mile off the Kupreanof Island shore until you reach the entrance to Portage Bay. You have come a bit more than 50 miles from Red Bluff Bay, and are started on your southern trek.

There is no law, of course, that says you have to hole up in Portage Bay. Thomas Bay is only 15 miles away and Petersburg itself is but 20 or so miles.

At any event, when you are ready to move on south, you have three possible routes to reach Ketchikan and/or the commencement of a clockwise tour of the Behm Canal. After emerging from the southern end of Wrangell Narrows (this time, keep the red aids to navigation on your port hand!), you can turn to port and take either (1) Zimovia Strait or (2) Stikine Strait, or you can swing to starboard for a run through (3) Snow Pass to reach Clarence Strait. I like the Zimovia trip because I wind up in Santa Anna Inlet with one more chance at the crabs there; Santa Anna Inlet is about 55 miles from the southern entrance to Wrangell Narrows and is a good day's run to the Ketchikan area. You should already have the chart necessary for Zimovia Strait (17385).

I never have done Stikine Strait, but it looks straight-forward enough and could be accomplished handily, I should think, with Chart 17382. Your goal might be Ratz Harbor, a fairly good anchorage and fishing spot notched into Prince of Wales Island; Chart 17360 will complete the course there and Chart 17423 will tuck you into it. Ratz Harbor is about 48 miles via Stikine Strait from Wrangell Narrows.

A slightly shorter, but more difficult route to Ratz Harbor from Wrangell Narrows (43 miles) is to carry around the western side of Zarembo Island through Snow Passage. Chart 17382 will warn you of the foul shores in the narrow passage, but it won't take care of the strong currents. Before trying Snow, you should check your current tables. The flood (which runs southeasterly) can reach 3.4 knots in the narrowest part and the ebb can be even stronger, a full 4 knots. Swirls are often present, and when a strong wind is in opposition to a vigorous current, steep waves are likely.

To enter Ratz Harbor, run in Clarence Strait until you have cleared the lighted aid to navigation that guards the northern shoulder of the entrance. The navigable entrance channel is less than 200 yards wide. Use your depthfinder and enter, then nudge along the eastern shore of the bay for about 500 yards to find a place for your pick in about six fathoms. Salmon fishing off the bay's entrance can be good. Ratz Harbor, a somewhat desolate place, is not a bad anchorage, and the Ketchikan area is less than a day's run from it.

Ratz, of course, is not the only resting place available. Many boaters, for example, like Myers Chuck, a dozen miles on to the south from Ratz on the eastern or mainland side, of Chatham Strait.

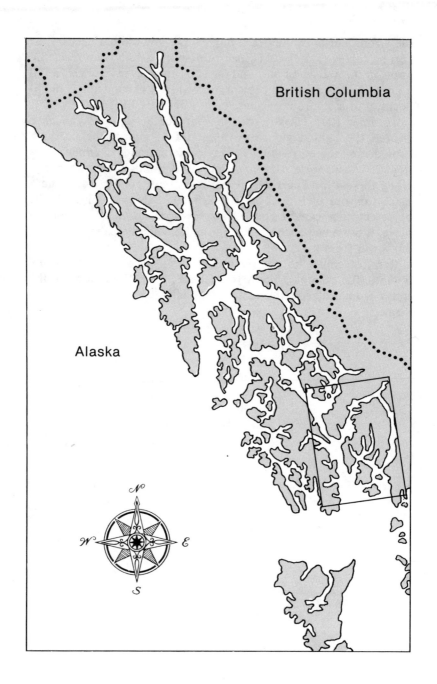

British Columbia

Alaska

The Behm Canal

You should have U.S. Charts 17422 (Western Part of Behm Canal; 1:79,334 scale) and 17424 (Eastern Part of Behm Canal; 1:80,000 scale).

Many boaters coming to Alaska 'do' the Behm Canal as their first excursion off the beaten path. There is nothing wrong with that, although they will backtrack after calling at Ketchikan, as they must do first to comply with U.S. Customs regulations. My treatment in this book of the Behm Canal as the final excursion of a Panhandle visit will enable the boater to 'do' the canal without any backtracking. Such a scheme, of course, eliminates a final stop at Ketchikan. That, I suppose, has its good and bad aspects. I mean no slight to the friendly folk in Ketchikan when I say that one visit to that port may be enough because it usually is a crowded, busy place in the summer with little available transient float space. For the boater who must fill a fuel tank, or replenish the food locker, my idea of bypassing Ketchikan, of course, is no good; backtracking then would be necessary. Well, you can't win 'em all. Anyway, here we go on a clockwise tour of the Behm Canal.

First, a word about the canal. It winds about 100 miles for three-fourths the distance around Revillagigedo Island, an interesting, large land mass that is 45 miles long and 30 miles wide. The other fourth of the complete circumnavigation would be in Revillagigedo Channel and Ketchikan's Tongass Narrows. The gorgeous and fantastic scenery to one side for just a moment, the Behm Canal itself, is a touring boater's paradise. Varying from ten miles wide to less than a half mile at one place it is remarkably free of navigation

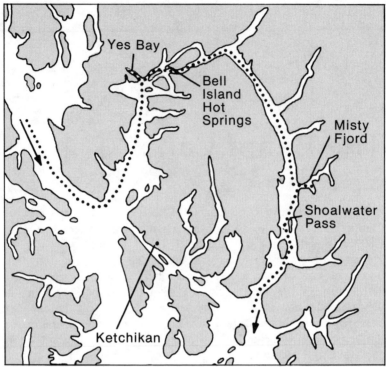

The Behm Canal

hazards. Although strong winds sometimes whistle through it in summer, it is replete with handy holes-in-the-wall in which one can hide in security. Some state of Washington boaters liken it to their own Hood Canal, but the Behm has many more hiding places. And tidal currents offer little challenge in Behm Canal; they mostly run at one or two knots on the maximum.

There are three places you 'must' visit in the Behm Canal—Yes Bay, the Bell Island Hot Springs, and Misty Fjord (the boater's lyrical name for Rudyerd Bay). There are a multitude of other spectacular and charming attractions. In this chapter, I'll show the way to those 'must' places, and will call to your attention some of the other attractions as we move along. How you pace yourself will be up to you.

Assuming that you have anchored overnight in Ratz Harbor, the western entrance to Behm Canal at Caamano Point is a 33-mile run south in Clarence Strait (I hope you haven't forgotten my earlier warning of potential adverse wind-and-current turmoil in Clarence). Move about a half-mile off Caamano as you swing to a northeasterly, then northerly, mid-channel course in Behm Canal to gain the entrance to Yes Bay, a bit more than 25 miles away.

If you have time, a pause in and near Naha Bay might result in a fish or two; it is a famed place for salmon, cod and halibut. Fishing is good throughout the Behm Canal, but you should be aware of restricted areas imposed for propagation reasons by Alaska state fishery officials. Two other excellent fishing opportunities present themselves near Yes Bay. One is a 50-fathom halibut bank two miles due east of Square Island in Spacious Bay; the skipper whose depthfinder can locate that one is likely to be well rewarded. The other is off Bluff Point, a choice spot for king salmon.

The best time to enter Yes Bay is at low water when hazards will be seen easily. Use the 1:40,000-scale blowup of Yes Bay on Chart 17422. Favor the northeastern shore as you move up to the community of Yes. There is a fishing resort and floats at Yes. Beyond it are two basins, both of which offer snug anchorages. Crawl closely along the northeastern shore near Yes to gain the first basin. Then, if you wish, turn sharply to port and, on a southeasterly heading, slip into an inviting bight for an eight-fathom anchorage. Or, if you'd rather, continue to crowd the northeastern shore and, hugging that shore as tight as you dare, slip through the very narrow entrance to the inner basin. Beware of foul ground to port as you do this. Take your pick of an anchorage that, probably, could defy a hurricane.

Bell Island Hot Springs is about a dozen miles to the east of Yes Bay. But, before you charge off in that direction, you should be advised that there is at least one delightfully tight anchorage in almost-hidden Klu Bay. It is about 11 miles from Yes Bay; to be safe, swing around the southern side of Gedney Island, move through Gedney Pass into Shrimp Bay (would it be profitable to wonder how it got its name?) and, finally, into the almost land-locked coziness of Klu Bay.

A deservedly-noted resort is at Bell Island Hot Springs. Its generous floats usually are capable of accommodating transients. Enjoy a healthful soak in the big pool; treat the crew to a good meal ashore.

It is a 45-mile run from the hot springs to Misty Fjord, but there is much to see and do en route. For example, there is a tight anchorage near the northern end of Anchor Pass, at the eastern end of Bell Island, but I don't think I'd try to tackle the pass itself; the low water controlling depth is only two feet and the current is strong. Walker Cove, 32 miles from the Hot Springs, is a seven-mile fjord of abrupt, almost perpendicular shores; indifferent anchorage is possible just inside the entrance. On the other side of the canal, however, is a better resting place in seven fathoms off the western side of the largest of the Snip Islands; entrance should be only from the north. A half-dozen miles more to the south on the western side of the canal is Manzanita Bay with a Forest Service float in the bight west of Wart Point.

Finally, there is Misty Fjord. There are 16 miles of fjord traversing, if you want to make the 'grand tour'. Or just here in the first inlet labeled Punchbowl Cove, is a mysterious and haunting place of precipitious sides, rock overhangs and beautiful waterfalls. Here perhaps is where Southeast Alaska, part of our nation's last frontier, will place its indelible, unforgettable stamp on your memory. It's possible to anchor overnight in Punchbowl Cove; the place to do it is near the head off the south shore.

But why do that when a much better anchorage is only about six miles to the south from the entrance of Misty Fjord in the north basin of Shoalwater Pass? The pass separates Winstanley Island from the mainland. To reach it safely, skirt to the west all of the New Eddystone Islands. At Slag Point, favor the mainland shore until the little wooded island to the west is cleared, then move over to anchor south of the island. Of course in getting to Shoalwater Pass, you will pass rather close to one of nature's great monoliths, the 230-foot New Eddystone Rock, right smack-dab in the middle of the Behm Canal and surely one more reminder that Southeast Alaska, indeed, is a fearful and wonderful place.

On a final and more practical note, there is the mundane fact that Dundas Island, perhaps your first stop in Canada on the way home, is just 60 miles from Shoalwater Pass. From the pass, it is only 20 miles south in Behm Canal to the familiar waters of Revillagigedo Channel.

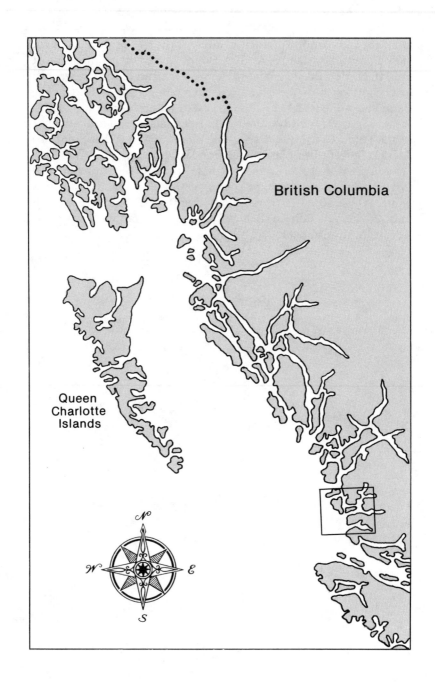

British Columbia

Queen
Charlotte
Islands

Going Home
(Via Fury Island)

You should have Canadian Chart 3779 (Entrance to Rivers Inlet; 1:36,500 scale).

Farewells, I think, are best when they are brief.

If this tome has been helpful in getting you to Southeast Alaska then, I hope, you'll use it with equal success on the southbound run to home. Every warning and caution with which I nagged you going north should apply in the other direction. And, perhaps, you'll want to reread pertinent chapters to remind yourself of the alternative anchorages that you weren't able to patronize going north. You can vary the southbound trip considerably by using some of them.

I have only one suggestion that varies markedly from the northbound route. It concerns your crossing of Queen Charlotte Sound. May I suggest that you might wish to employ a place called Fury Island as your jumping-off spot? It not only is situated ideally for such duty, but is an absolutely charming place to boot.

If you will recall, this book suggested that you anchor in Pruth Bay at the northern end of Calvert Island after crossing Queen Charlotte Sound northbound. Trouble is, for a southbound crossing, Pruth Bay, 20 miles north of the southern end of Calvert Island, hardly is a 'jumping off' place. From Pruth Bay, you'd have a two or three-hour run before you could begin to decide whether conditions were right for a crossing. Fury Island will rescue you from that situation.

To reach Fury, move south in Fitz Hugh Sound past the entrance to Pruth Bay and get over to within 400 yards or so of the Adden-

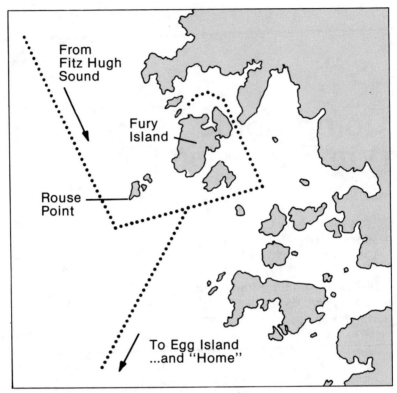

Fury Island—A Jump To Home

broke Island light. From there, my chart shows I steered 155° true for 8.3 miles until I had Rouse Point abeam to port about 500 yards off. Then, slowing down with depthfinder on and Chart 3779 at the ready, I steered 079° true for one mile or until I could look abaft the port beam to see the channel separating Fury and Penrose Islands. At that point, I turned abruptly to port; my chart says I steered 325° true to slip through the pass. Once inside the land-locked cove, I turned again to port and found secure anchorage in about four fathoms. The anchorage, if chosen correctly, will give you a close view of a beautiful, wooded, white clam shell beach, and a longer view right smack into Queen Charlotte Sound. Just sit there, my friend, and look. When the crossing appears right for you, go. When I decided to leave, my chart shows that, from the south end of Fury Island, I steered 197° true for 6.9 miles to come abeam to port of the Dugout Rocks light. From there, it was just a matter of joining the regular crossing route, either to Blunden Harbour or God's Pocket. Yes, Fury Island could be used on a north-bound run, but I don't think a northbound skipper, perhaps tired and apprehensive from a tumultuous trip, is psychologically prepared to ferret out Fury Island; Pruth Bay, I think, is easier on the northbound trip.

Well, as I say, the best farewell is brief.

My farewell to you, Skipper, is begun by quoting something from the very first chapter of this book: "You see, I believe that much that is written fails to recognize that there are many thousands of boaters who are not experienced and who, thus, remain timid when it comes to the dream of cruising to Alaska. They are not cowards. There is a big, big difference between being timid and being a coward. A coward lacks courage. A timid person only needs self-confidence ..."

Well, Skipper, you've made it to the Land of the Midnight Sun. You've done something few other pleasureboaters accomplish. Congratulations! And I have news for you.

You no longer are inexperienced.

You have gained a self-confidence you'll never lose.

And you have a million memories.

For the most part, it went all right, didn't it?

Without rocking the boat?

Too much?

Appendix I
Charts Used in this Book

Arranged in northbound sequence by geographical groups
(United States charts, 5 numerals; Canadian charts, 4 numerals)
As of June 1, 1987

Required Chart Number	Helpful Chart Number	Official Title of Chart	Scale	Chapter Numbers In Book
		Olympia to Bedwell Harbour		
18448		Puget Sound, Seattle to Olympia	1:80,000	5
18441		Admiralty Inlet & Puget Sound to Seattle	1:80,000	6
18421		Strait of Juan de Fuca to Strait of Georgia	1:80,000	6, 7
	18427	Anacortes to Skagit Bay	1:25,000	7
	18434	San Juan Channel	1:25,000	7
		Bedwell Harbour to Nanaimo		
L/C3462		Strait of Juan de Fuca to Strait of Georgia	1:80,000	8
L/C3463		Strait of Georgia, Southern Portion	1:80,000	8, 9
3441		Haro Strait, Boundary Pass and Satellite Channel	1:40,000	8
3442		North Pender Island to Thetis Island	1:40,000	8
3443		Thetis Island to Nanaimo	1:40,000	8
		Nanaimo to Minstrel Island		
L/C3512		Strait of Georgia, Central Portion	1:80,000	9, 10
L/C3513		Strait of Georgia, Northern Portion	1:80,000	10
3538		Desolation Sound and Sutil Channel	1:40,000	10, 11
3539		Discovery Passage	1:40,000	10, 11
3541		Approaches to Toba Inlet	1:40,000	10
3543		Cordero Channel	1:40,000	10, 11
3544		Johnstone Strait, Race Passage and Current Passage	1:25,000	12
3545		Johnstone Strait, Port Neville to Robson Bight	1:40,000	12
		Crossing Queen Charlotte Strait and Sound		
		(*via God's Pocket)		
		(**via Blunden Harbour)		
3568		Johnstone Strait, Western Portion	1:36,500	12, 13
3569*		Broughton Strait	1:37,600	13
3597*		Pulteney Point to Egg Island	1:73,000	13
3776		Smith Sound and approaches	1:37,100	13
3727		Cape Calvert to Goose Island, including Fitz Hugh Sound	1:73,600	13, 14
3525**		Tribune Channel	1:37,500	13

173

Required Chart Number	Helpful Chart Number	Official Title of Chart	Scale	Chapter Numbers In Book
3576**		Fife Sound and Kingcome Inlet	1:37,500	13
3570**		Wells Passage and adjacent channels	1:37,500	13
3574**		Numas Islands to Harris Island	1:37,400	13
3561**		Harbours in Broughton & Queen Charlotte Straits	Blunden Harbour 1:12,200	13
3551**		Jeannette Islands to Cape Caution	1:40,000	13
	3797**	Plans in Vicinity of Queen Charlotte & Fitz Hugh Sounds	Allison Harbour 1:18,200	13

Pruth Bay to Prince Rupert

3785		Namu Harbour to Dryad Point	1:40,500	14
3720		Idol Point to Ocean Falls	1:41,100	14
3728		Milbanke Sound and approaches	1:76,600	14, 15
3710		Plans in the Vicinity of Laredo and Milbanke Sounds	Reid Passage 1:18,900	14, 15
3734		Jorkins Point to Sarah Island	1:36,000	15
3738		Sarah Island to Swanson Bay	1:35,800	15
3739		Swanson Bay to Work Island	1:35,600	15
3740		Work Island to Point Cummings	1:35,500	16
3742		Otter Passage to McKay Reach	1:70,900	16
3772		Grenville Channel, Sainty Point to Baker Inlet	1:36,200	16, 17
3773		Grenville Channel, Baker Inlet to Ogden Channel	1:36,500	17
3927		Bonila Island to Edye Passage	1:77,800	17
3957		Approaches to Prince Rupert Harbour	1:40,000	17, 18

Crossing Dixon Entrance

3955		Plans - Prince Rupert Harbour Area	1:10,000	18
3959		Hudson Bay Passage	1:40,000	18
3992		Approaches to Portland Inlet	1:40,000	18
17434		Revillagigedo Channel	1:80,000	19
17428		Revillagigedo Channel, Nichols Passage & Tongass Narrows	1:40,000	19, 21

Ketchikan to Juneau

17420		Hecate Strait to Etolin Island	1:229,376	21
17385		Ernest Sound—Eastern Passage and Zimovia Strait	1:80,000	21, 22, 30

Required Chart Number	Helpful Chart Number	Official Title of Chart	Scale	Chapter Numbers In Book
	17423	Harbor Charts—Clarence Strait and Behm Canal	Myers Chuck 1:40,000	21, 30
17382		Zarembo Island and Approaches	1:80,000	22, 23, 30
17375		Wrangell Narrows	1:20,000	23, 30
	17367	Thomas, Farragut & Portage Bays	1:40,000	23, 30
17360		Etolin Island to Midway Islands	1:217,828	23, 24 25, 30
17363		Pybus, Hobart & Windham Bays	1:40,000	24
17300		Stephens Passage to Cross Sound	1:209,978	25, 28
17315		Gastineau Channel and Taku Inlet	1:40,000	25, 27

Skagway and Funter Bay

17316		Lynn Canal, from Icy Strait to Point Sherman	1:80,000	27, 28
17317		Lynn Canal-Point Sherman to Skagway	1:80,000	27

Glacier Bay and Tenakee Springs

17302		Icy Strait and Cross Sound·	1:80,000	28
17318		Glacier Bay	1:80,000	28

Sitka

17320		Coronation Island to Lisianski Strait	1:217,828	29, 30
17338		Peril Strait	1:40,000	29
17323		Salisbury Sound and Peril Strait	1:40,000	29
17324		Sitka Sound to Salisbury Sound	1:40,000	29
17327		Sitka Harbor	1:10,000	29

Chatham Strait Harbors

17337		Harbors in Chatham Strait and Vicinity	Warm Spring Bay 1:20,000	30
17336		Harbors in Chatham Strait and Vicinity	Red Bluff Bay 1:20,000	30

Behm Canal

17422		Western Part of Behm Canal	1:79,334	31
17424		Eastern Part of Behm Canal	1:80,000	31

Re-Crossing Queen Charlotte Sound

3779		Entrance to Rivers Inlet	1:36,500	32

Appendix II
Moorages, Anchorages Identified In This Book

Arranged alphabetically
(General location: WA, Washington; BC, British Columbia; AK, Alaska)

Name of Harbor	Chapter Number In Book	General Location	Float Moorage	Anchorage	Chart Numbers
● Alert Bay	13	BC	X		3569
● Allies Island	10	BC		X	3594
● Anan Bay	22	AK		X	17385
● Anchor Pass	31	AK		X	17422
● Anita Bay	22	AK		X	17382
● Appleton Cove	29	AK		X	17338
● Baker Inlet	17	BC		X	3772
● Ballet Bay	10	BC		X	L/C3512
● Bartlett Cove	28	AK		X	17318
● Beaumont Marine Park	7	BC		X	18421, 3452
● Bedwell Harbour	7	BC	X		3452, L/C3462
● Bell Island Hot Springs	31	AK	X		17422
● Berg Bay	22	AK		X	17385
● Bickley Bay	11	BC		X	3539
● Blake Island	5	WA	X	X	18448
● Blind Channel	11	BC	X		3539
● Blunden Harbour	13	BC		X	3561
● Brundige Inlet	18	BC		X	3959
● Burial Cove	12	BC		X	3569
● Butedale	15	BC	X		3739
● Cannery Cove	24	AK		X	17363
● Cleveland Passage	24	AK		X	17360
● Copeland Islands	10	BC		X	3539
● Cornet Bay	6	WA	X	X	18421, 18427
● Cutter Cove	12	BC		X	3545
● Deep Bay	29	AK		X	17323
● Deer Harbor	7	WA	X		18434
● Dockton (see Quarter-master Harbor)					
● Double Island	7	WA		X	18434
● Douglas	25	AK	X		17315

● Eagle Harbor	6	WA	X	X	18441
● Echo Bay	27	AK		X	17316
● Edmonds	6	WA	X		18441
● Elger Bay	6	WA		X	18441
● Entrance Island	24	AK	X		17363
● Fannie Cove	14	BC		X	3785
● Fanny Bay	11	BC		X	3541
● Filucy Bay	5	WA	X	X	18448
● Foggy Bay	19	AK		X	17434
● Fords Terror	25	AK		X	17360
● Forward Harbour	12	BC		X	3544
● Friday Harbor	7	WA	X		18421, 18434
● Funter Bay	27	AK	X	X	17316
● Fury Island	32	BC		X	3551
● Galley Bay	10	BC		X	3541
● Gig Harbor	5	WA	X	X	18448
● God's Pocket	13	BC		X	3569
● Haines	27	AK	X		17317
● Ham Island	19	AK		X	17428
● Jedediah Island	9	BC		X	L/C3512
● Jones Cove	13	BC		X	3785
● Jones Island	7	WA	X	X	18421, 18434
● Juneau	25	AK	X		17315
● Kah Shakes Cove	19	AK		X	17434
● Ketchikan	19	AK	X		17428
● Khutze Inlet	15	BC		X	3739
● Kingston	6	WA	X		18441
● Klu Bay	31	AK		X	17422
● Kumealon Inlet	17	BC		X	3773
● Kynumpt Harbour	14	BC		X	3720
● LaConner	6	WA	X		18421, 18427
● Lagoon Cove	12	BC	X		3545
● Longbranch (see Filucy Bay)					
● Lowe Inlet	16	BC		X	3772
● Lund	10	BC	X		L/C3513
● Manzanita Bay	31	AK		X	17424
● Melanie Cove	10	BC		X	3594
● Mink Island	10	BC		X	3594
● Minstrel Island	12	BC	X		3567
● Misty Fjord	31	AK		X	17424
● Montague Harbour	8	BC		X	3538
● Myers Chuck	21	AK	X	X	17385, 17423

● Nanaimo	8	BC	X	X	3443
● Nismeni Cove	29	AK		X	17338
● Oak Harbor	6	WA	X		18441
● Oliver Cove	14	BC		X	3710
● Orcas	7	WA	X		18434
● Pender Harbour	9	BC	X	X	L/C3512
● Penn Cove	6	WA	X	X	18441
● Petersburg	23	AK	X		17375
● Pirate's Cove	8	BC		X	3443
● Portage Bay	23	AK		X	17360, 17367
● Port Hardy	13	BC	X		3597
● Port Madison	6	WA		X	18441
● Potts Lagoon	12	BC		X	3568
● Powell River (see Westview)					
● Prideaux Haven	10	BC		X	3538
● Prince Rupert	17	BC	X		3957
● Pruth Bay	13	BC		X	3797
● Punchbowl Cove (see Misty Fjord)					
● Quartermaster Harbor	5	WA	X	X	18448
● Ratz Harbor	30	AK		X	17360, 17423
● Red Bluff Bay	30	AK		X	17336
● Refuge Cove	10	BC	X	X	3538
● Reid Inlet	28	AK		X	17318
● Rescue Bay	15	BC		X	3734
● Roche Harbor	7	WA	X		18421
● Rosario	7	WA	X		18421
● Rudyerd Bay (see Misty Fjord)					
● Sanford Cove	25	AK		X	17360
● Santa Anna Inlet	21	AK		X	17385
● Saook Bay	29	AK		X	17338
● Schulze Cove	29	AK		X	17323
● Seattle	6	WA	X		18441
● Secret Cove	9	BC	X	X	L/C3512
● Shearwater	14	BC	X		3785
● Shoal Bay	11	BC	X		3539
● Shoalwater Pass	31	AK		X	17424
● Sitka	29	AK	X		17327
● Skagway	27	AK	X		17317
● Smuggler Cove	9	BC		X	L/C3513
● Snip Islands	31	AK		X	17424

● Squaxin Island	5	WA	X	X	18448
● Squirrel Cove	10	BC	X	X	3538
● Squitty Bay	9	BC	X		L/C3513
● Stuart Island	7	WA	X	X	18421
● Sturt Bay	10	BC		X	L/C3513
● Sullivan Bay	13	BC	X		3570
● Sullivan Island	27	AK		X	17317
● Taku Harbor	25	AK	X	X	17300
● Telegraph Harbour	8	BC	X	X	3442
● Tenakee Springs	28	AK	X		17300
● Tenedos Bay	10	BC		X	3538
● Tent Island	8	BC		X	3442
● Thomas Bay	23	AK		X	17360, 17367
● Troup Harbour	14	BC		X	3720
● Walker Cove	31	AK		X	17424
● Walsh Cove	10	BC		X	3538
● Warm Spring Bay	30	AK	X	X	17337
● Westview	10	BC	X		L/C3513
● Woewodski Island	23	AK		X	17375
● Woodpecker Cove	22	AK		X	17382
● Wrangell	22	AK	X		17382
● Yes Bay	31	AK	X	X	17422